**SECOND EDITION**

# STEP FORWARD

**4**

## STANDARDS-BASED LANGUAGE LEARNING
## FOR WORK AND ACADEMIC READINESS

SERIES DIRECTOR
**Jayme Adelson-Goldstein**

**Barbara R. Denman**

**OXFORD**
UNIVERSITY PRESS

# TABLE OF CONTENTS

**Step Forward** supports learners as they work to meet the *English Language Proficiency Standards for Adult Education* (ELPS) and the *College and Career Readiness Standards for Adult Education* (CCRS). See *Step Forward*'s **Teacher Resource Center** for step-by-step lesson plans that list the level-specific ELP and CCR standards, and for other detailed correlations.

| LANGUAGE STRATEGIES | | COLLEGE & CAREER READINESS | |
|---|---|---|---|
| **Reading & Writing** | **Listening & Speaking** | **Critical Thinking** | **Collaboration** |
| ■ Read a conversation | **Conversation**<br>■ Practice with greetings<br>**Focused Listening**<br>■ Listen for countries | **Critical thinking**<br>■ Process instructions | ■ Understand teamwork<br>■ Communicate information<br>■ Communicate verbally |
| ■ Read an article about test anxiety<br>■ Read a graph and a note<br>■ Write a paragraph about your learning style<br>**Writing strategy**<br>■ Understanding main idea vs. examples<br>**Reading strategy**<br>■ Understanding how to use bullets and bullet points<br>■ Reading complex charts and texts several time | **Conversation**<br>■ Express opinions about education<br>■ Disagree politely<br>**Focused Listening**<br>■ Listen for action and stative verbs<br>■ Listen for personality words<br>**Pronunciation**<br>■ Practice *t* sounds | **Critical thinking**<br>■ Locate information<br>■ Infer information<br>■ Analyze information<br>**Problem solving**<br>■ Determine how to talk with your roommates about a problem | ■ Understand teamwork<br>■ Work with others<br>■ Solve problems<br>■ Manage time |
| ■ Read an article about the news<br>■ Write a news story<br>**Writing strategy**<br>■ Using adverbial time clauses for sequencing<br>**Reading strategy**<br>■ Understanding the purpose of illustrations | **Conversation**<br>■ Talk about a current event<br>■ Express agreement<br>■ Question and restate<br>■ Give your opinion<br>**Focused Listening**<br>■ Listen for details<br>**Pronunciation**<br>■ Using word stress | **Critical thinking**<br>■ Differentiate between fact and opinion<br>**Problem solving**<br>■ Determine how to join in a discussion about current events | ■ Listen actively<br>■ Cooperate with others<br>■ Give your opinion in a group<br>■ Understand teamwork<br>■ Work with others<br>■ Communicate information |
| ■ Read an article about transportation<br>■ Write about a bad phone experience<br>■ Read a graph and text<br>**Writing strategy**<br>■ Using a comma and quotes to repeat a speaker's words<br>**Reading strategy**<br>■ Annotating a text<br>■ Understanding chart labels | **Conversation**<br>■ Use reported speech<br>■ Make travel plans<br>■ Make suggestions<br>**Focused Listening**<br>■ Listen for reported speech<br>■ Listen for details about a message system<br>■ Listen to a staff meeting<br>**Pronunciation**<br>■ Practice pronunciation of the letter *s* | **Critical thinking**<br>■ Discuss the difference between *ask* and *tell*<br>■ Listen and decide on the solutions to problems and the consequences of the solutions<br>**Problem solving**<br>■ Identify ways to solve a scheduling conflict<br>■ Read issues and make suggestions<br>■ Decide how to allocate money | ■ Listen actively<br>■ Work independently<br>■ Cooperate with others<br>■ Communicate verbally<br>■ Locate information |

| LANGUAGE STRATEGIES | | COLLEGE & CAREER READINESS | |
|---|---|---|---|
| **Reading & Writing** | **Listening & Speaking** | **Critical Thinking** | **Collaboration** |
| ■ Write an essay about the importance of money<br>■ Read about financial planning<br>■ Read a pie chart and a note<br>**Writing strategy**<br>■ Using prompts in formal essays<br>**Reading strategy**<br>■ Using evidence and reasons to support a writer's point | **Conversation**<br>■ Negotiate and compromise on a budget<br>■ Make a suggestion to negotiate and compromise<br>■ Talk about ways to save money<br>■ Build consensus<br>**Focused Listening**<br>■ Listen to a credit counseling session<br>■ Listen to small business owners discussing their future<br>**Pronunciation**<br>■ Pausing at commas | **Critical thinking**<br>■ Decide why it's important to save money<br>**Problem solving**<br>■ Decide how to talk to a friend about poor spending habits | ■ Work independently<br>■ Understand teamwork<br>■ Work with others<br>■ Locate information<br>■ Communicate information<br>■ Communicate verbally<br>■ Listen actively<br>■ Analyze information<br>■ Understand budgets<br>■ Solve problems |
| ■ Read an email<br>■ Write an email about purchase problems<br>■ Read an article about consumer protections<br>■ Read a pie chart<br>**Writing strategy**<br>■ Using words to help the reader identify important information<br>**Reading strategy**<br>■ Using context to understand new words<br>■ Understand a pie chart | **Conversation**<br>■ Report problems with services<br>■ Apologize<br>■ Keep a conversation on topic<br>**Focused Listening**<br>■ Listen to return instructions<br>■ Listen for different solutions to a work problem<br>**Pronunciation**<br>■ Linking words | **Critical thinking**<br>■ Interpret a pie chart and a note<br>**Problem solving**<br>■ Determine how to complain about a yard sale purchase | ■ Listen actively<br>■ Understand teamwork<br>■ Communicate information<br>■ Work with others<br>■ Cooperate with others<br>■ Work with others<br>■ Convey information in writing |
| ■ Write a blog post about a health issue<br>■ Read about choosing health insurance<br>■ Read about weather conditions<br>**Writing strategy**<br>■ Using parentheses or definitions to define words or terms<br>**Reading strategy**<br>■ Using Frequently Asked Questions (FAQs) to organize information and help the reader<br>■ Reading tables | **Conversation**<br>■ Talk about your opinions about health issues<br>■ Ask and answer questions at a medical visit<br>■ Confirm advice<br>**Focused Listening**<br>■ Listen for different forms of advice<br>■ Listen for details about a workplace injury and treatment<br>■ Listen to advice about using a computer<br>**Pronunciation**<br>■ Pronunciation of *s* and *ch* in different words | **Critical thinking**<br>■ Determine the strongest advice<br>■ Determine the health precautions different kinds of workers should take<br>■ Analyze different types of medical insurance<br>**Problem solving**<br>■ Decide how to give advice on health to a loved one | ■ Understand teamwork<br>■ Cooperate with others<br>■ Communicate information<br>■ Work with others<br>■ Communicate verbally<br>■ Understand graphs and tables<br>■ Solve problems<br>■ Analyze information |

**"What's new?"** is a question that often greets the arrival of a second edition, but let's start with the similarities between *Step Forward Second Edition* and its predecessor. This edition retains the original's effective instructional practices for teaching adult English language learners, such as focusing on learner outcomes, learner-centered lessons, thematic four-skill integration with associated vocabulary, direct instruction of grammar and pronunciation, focused listening, and sourced texts. It also preserves the instructional flexibility that allows it to be used in classes that meet twice a week, and those that meet every day. Perhaps most significantly, this edition continues to provide the differentiation support for teachers in multilevel settings.

The *College and Career Readiness Standards for Adult Education* (Pimentel, 2013) and the 2016 *English Language Proficiency Standards* echo the research by ACT, Parrish and Johnson, Wrigley, and others linking critical thinking skills, academic language, and language strategies to learners' academic success and employability. Rigorous language instruction is key to accelerating our learners' transition into family-sustaining jobs, civic engagement, and/or post-secondary education. *Step Forward Second Edition* has integrated civic, college, and career readiness skills in every lesson. Each *Step Forward* author considered adult learners' time constraints while crafting lessons that flow from objective to outcome, encouraging and challenging learners with relevant tasks that ensure their growth.

## *STEP FORWARD* KEY CONCEPTS

Our learners' varied proficiency levels, educational backgrounds, goals, and interests make the English language classroom a remarkable place. They also create some instructional challenges. To ensure that your learners leave class having made progress toward their language and life goals, these key concepts underpin the *Step Forward* curriculum.

Effective instruction…

▶ acknowledges and makes use of learners' prior knowledge and critical thinking skills.

▶ helps learners develop the language that allows them to demonstrate their 21st century skills.

▶ contextualizes lessons to support learners' workplace, career, and civic goals.

▶ ensures that each lesson's learning objectives, instructions, and tasks are clear.

▶ differentiates instruction in order to accommodate learners at varying proficiency levels within the same class.

▶ provides informational text (including graphs, charts, and images) that builds and expands learners' knowledge.

## *STEP FORWARD* COMPONENTS

Each level of *Step Forward* correlates to *The Oxford Picture Dictionary*. Each *Step Forward* level includes the following components:

### *Step Forward* Student Book
Twelve thematic units focusing on everyday adult topics, each with six lessons integrating communication, workplace, and academic skills, along with language strategies for accuracy and fluency.

### *Step Forward* Audio Program
The recorded vocabulary, focused listening, conversations, pronunciation, and reading materials from the *Step Forward* Student Book.

### *Step Forward* Workbook
Practice exercises for independent work in the classroom or as homework, as well as "Do the Math" sections.

### *Step Forward* Teacher Resource Center
An online collection of downloadable resources that support the *Step Forward* program. The *Step Forward* Teacher Resource Center contains the following components:

• *Step Forward* Lesson Plans: an instructional planning resource with detailed, step-by-step lesson plans featuring multilevel teaching strategies and teaching tips

• *Step Forward* Multilevel Activities: over 100 communicative practice activities and 72 picture cards; lesson materials that work equally well in single-level or multilevel settings

• *Step Forward* Multilevel Grammar Exercises: multilevel grammar practice for the structures presented in the *Step Forward* Student Book

• *Step Forward* Testing Program: tests for every unit in the *Step Forward* Student Book

• *Step Forward* Literacy Reproducible Activities: literacy activities that correspond to the *Step Forward Introductory Level* Student Book, intended to support pre-beginning or semi-literate level learners

• Correlations: correlations to national standards, including the *College and Career Readiness Standards* and the *English Language Proficiency Standards*

• *Step Forward* Answer Keys and Audio Scripts for the *Step Forward* Student Book and Workbook

### *Step Forward* Classroom Presentation Tool
On-screen *Step Forward* Student Book pages, including audio at point of use and whole-class interactive activities, transform each Student Book into a media-rich classroom presentation tool in order to maximize-heads up learning. The intuitive, book-on-screen design helps teachers navigate easily from page to page.

I know I speak for the authors and the entire *Step Forward* publishing team when I say it's a privilege to serve you and your learners.

*Jayme Adelson-Goldstein*

Jayme Adelson-Goldstein, Series Director

## WELCOME, LEARNERS!

**Learning English is a challenge. *Step Forward* can help. Here are some ideas to try.**

Congratulations on continuing your English language studies! Learning English can be a challenge, but it is also an opportunity. In every *Step Forward* lesson, you will talk to and work with interesting people — your classmates. Each time you collaborate with a partner or team, you improve your communication skills. This will help you in the workplace and in your community. *Step Forward* also helps you improve your academic skills so you can succeed in high school diploma classes, career training, and college courses.

These five ideas can help you as you learn new strategies to listen, speak, read, and write well in English.

## STUDY THE LISTS, CHARTS, AND NOTES IN *STEP FORWARD*

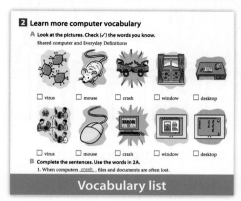

**Vocabulary list**

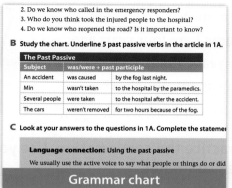

**Grammar chart**

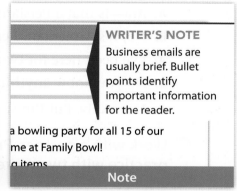

**Note**

▸ Record new words in a notebook, index cards, or on your digital device. Write their definitions and translations. Write a phrase or sentence with the new word.

▸ The grammar charts help you analyze the structure of English. Study them carefully. Look for the patterns in the examples.

▸ Notes help you communicate more accurately and fluently. For example, this note teaches you about writing and reading business emails.

## ASK QUESTIONS TO BUILD YOUR KNOWLEDGE

When you want more information, ask a question. Did you hear something you didn't understand? Ask for clarification. When you read, ask yourself questions.

## BE BRAVE IN CLASS TO PRACTICE SPEAKING

Take risks. It's okay to be nervous, but don't let it stop you! Breathe deeply, and raise your hand. Volunteer to answer a question, act out a conversation, or give a report. Your confidence will grow.

## TAKE NOTES TO HELP YOU STUDY

Did your teacher give you a handout? Circle the new words and underline important information. During the lesson, use a notebook or a cell phone app to record your ideas, questions, and new vocabulary. Study your notes to help you remember the lesson.

## FOCUS ON YOUR GOALS TO PERSIST

Sometimes it's hard to come to class. Other times it's hard to find time to study. When that happens, take a moment to remember why you want to learn English.

# The First Step

Sep-6-23

## 1 Get to know your classmates

**A** Look at the picture. What are the people talking about? How do you know?

🔊 1-02 **B** Listen and read the conversation. Where are Ara and Estela from?

A: Excuse me. Is anyone sitting here?

B: No. Someone was sitting here, but she left. Have a seat!

A: Thanks. I'm Estela, by the way.

B: Hi, Estela. I'm Ara.

A: Ara—is that a Persian name?

B: No, it's Armenian. I came here four years ago.

A: I've been here for two years. I'm from El Salvador.

B: Do you know anything about this class?

A: Not really. But I'm sure we'll learn a lot!

**C** Work with a partner. Practice the conversation. Use your own information. Then practice with two more classmates.

## 2 Review verb tenses

**A** Study the sentences and the time lines. Complete the charts with the verb tenses from the box.

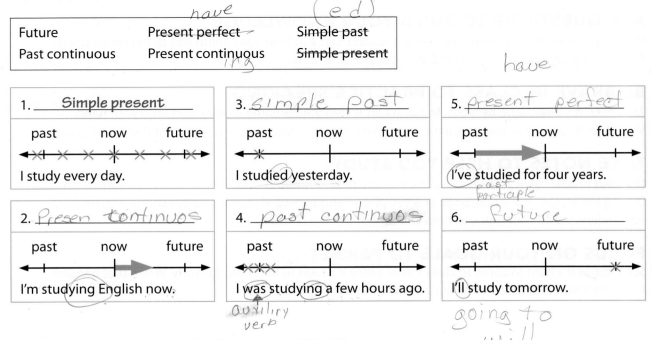

have (ed)

| | | |
|---|---|---|
| Future | Present perfect | Simple past |
| Past continuous | Present continuous | Simple present |

ing

have

1. __Simple present__

| past | now | future |
|---|---|---|
I study every day.

2. __Presen continuos__

| past | now | future |
|---|---|---|
I'm studying English now.

3. __simple past__

| past | now | future |
|---|---|---|
I studied yesterday.

auxiliry verb

4. __past continuos__

| past | now | future |
|---|---|---|
I was studying a few hours ago.

5. __present perfect__

| past | now | future |
|---|---|---|
I've studied for four years.

past partiaple

6. __Future__

| past | now | future |
|---|---|---|
I'll study tomorrow.

going to will

**B** Work with a partner. Identify the verb tense in each question. Then ask and answer the questions.

1. What are you thinking about right now? *Present Cont*
2. What do you usually do after class?
3. How long have you studied English? *past*
4. What did you do last weekend? *past simp*
5. Where will you speak English this week?

# 3 Word families

**A** Look at the chart. Complete the sentences.

| Word | Part of speech | Word | Part of speech |
|------|----------------|------|----------------|
| study | verb (v) | studious | adjective (adj.) |
| student | noun (n) | studiously | adverb (adv.) |

1. Sara is a part-time ___student___ .
2. She _____ every night after work.
3. She spends a lot of time on her homework. She's really _____ .
4. She's working _____ right now because she has an exam tomorrow.

**B** Use a dictionary to find the word family for the word *help*. Complete the chart.

| Word | Part of speech | Example |
|------|----------------|---------|
| help | noun | I like this dictionary a lot. It's a big __help__ . |
| | verb | I think this class will really _____ me. |
| | adjective | Our teacher is friendly and very _____ . |
| | adverb | Ara _____ gave me his extra pen. |

**C** Work with a partner. Use a dictionary to find another word family. Complete the chart.

| Word | Part of speech | Example |
|------|----------------|---------|
| | | |
| | | |
| | | |
| | | |

**D** Talk about your word family with your classmates.

# It Takes All Kinds!

A LOOK AT
- Personalities and learning styles
- Action and stative verbs
- Asking for help to understand

## LESSON 1 VOCABULARY

### 1 Identify personality and talent vocabulary

**A** Collaborate with your classmates to complete each task.

1. Brainstorm words your classmates use to describe their personalities.
2. Identify the types of people you find it easiest to get along with. State and discuss your reasons.

**B** Work with a partner. Mark the chart.

| Vocabulary | I know it | My partner knows it | We need to learn it |
|---|---|---|---|
| a. adventurous | | | |
| b. athletic | | | |
| c. musical | | | |
| d. social | | | |
| e. artistic | | | |
| f. mathematical | | | |
| g. quiet | | | |
| h. verbal | | | |

**C** Continue to work with your partner. Match each question with the vocabulary from 1B.

___h___ 1. Which type of person enjoys words and talking with others?

_____ 2. Which type of person is good with numbers?

_____ 3. Which type of person is good at sports?

_____ 4. Which personality type loves being around people?

_____ 5. What is a person who doesn't speak very often called?

_____ 6. If you are good at singing or playing an instrument, what type of person are you?

_____ 7. If you are good at drawing or painting, what type of person are you?

_____ 8. If you love travel and trying new things, which adjective describes you?

**VOCABULARY NOTE**

Look for words that are related to the new words you want to learn.

🔊 **D** Listen for information about personality types. Check your work in 1C.
1-03

🔊 **E** Listen again. Take notes on the people, their personalities, and the things they like to do or are good at. Report what you heard.
1-03

# 2 Learn about learning styles

**A** Look at the learning styles website. Complete the chart with information about the people in the pictures.

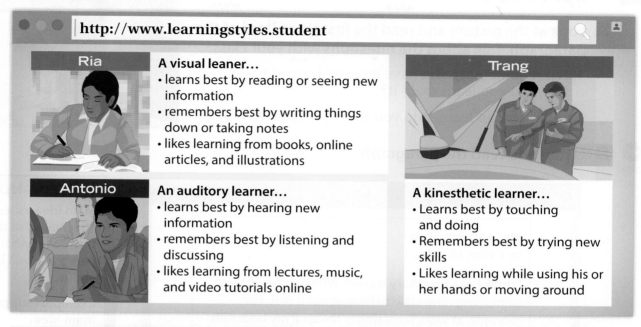

http://www.learningstyles.student

**Ria**

**A visual leaner…**
- learns best by reading or seeing new information
- remembers best by writing things down or taking notes
- likes learning from books, online articles, and illustrations

**Trang**

**A kinesthetic learner…**
- Learns best by touching and doing
- Remembers best by trying new skills
- Likes learning while using his or her hands or moving around

**Antonio**

**An auditory learner…**
- learns best by hearing new information
- remembers best by listening and discussing
- likes learning from lectures, music, and video tutorials online

| Name | Learning style | When there is a computer problem… |
|---|---|---|
| | | Calls a friend for advice |
| | | Tries to fix the problem |
| | | Reads the instruction manual |

**B** Work with a partner. Practice the conversation. Use the words in 2A.

A: *What kind of learner are you?*

B: *I think I'm an auditory learner. I like learning from lectures. What about you?*

**C** Conduct research with a team. Look online, and/or survey your classmates in order to report on the questions below.

How can you find out what type of learner you are? What type of learner is each person in your group? What advice would you give each type of learner?

**D** Report the results of your research.

*Our team found _____ to help you figure out what type of learner you are. Our group has _____ and _____ learners. We think that _____ learners should …*

---

## ▶▶TEST YOURSELF

Work with a partner. Take turns reading and responding to the prompts in 1C.

**Partner A:** Read prompts 1–4. Partner B: Listen and write the vocabulary words.
**Partner B:** Read prompts 5–8. Partner A: Listen and write the vocabulary words.

# 1 Prepare to write

**A** Look at the picture and read the first three lines of the paragraph. Talk about the questions with your class.

1. Name something you have recently learned to do. How did you learn to do it?

2. What kind of learner do you think you are? Why?

1-04

**B** Listen and read the paragraph.

> ### My Learning Style
> by Carlos Morales
>
> I think I'm an auditory learner. When I have to learn something new, I like to hear about it first. For example, at work I remember things if my boss tells me about them, but I often forget information if I read it in an email. At home, I don't spend much time reading online or in the newspaper. I prefer to watch the news on TV or listen on the radio. When I'm cooking or doing housework, I like to listen to interviews on radio talk shows. Sometimes I learn a lot from them. In class, I understand best when I hear new information from the teacher, and then talk about it with the people in my class. I don't learn very well from independent reading in a lab. I'm really social and I like brainstorming and working with a group. My goal is to be a counselor for young people some day, so being a good listener is really important to me.

**WRITER'S NOTE**

**Main idea vs. examples**
The main idea tells the reader what the paragraph will be about.

**Examples support the main idea.**
Use examples to give the reader more information about your main idea.

**C** Study the paragraph. Answer the questions.

1. What is the main idea of Carlos' paragraph?

_____

2. What are some examples Carlos uses to support his main idea?

_____

3. What is Carlos' career goal? How do his learning style and his goal connect?

_____

## 2 Plan and write

**A** Talk about the questions with your class. Take notes.

1. How are you similar to the writer in 1B?

2. How are you different from the writer in 1B?

**B** Write a paragraph about your learning style. Use the model paragraph in 1B and your answers to the questions in 2A.

My Learning Style

By _____

I think that I…
For example, …
When I'm…, I like to…
In class, I understand best…
I'm really… and… I like/don't like…
My goal…

## 3 Get feedback and revise

**A** Use the editing checklist to review your writing. Check (✓) the true sentences.

☐ I began with my main idea.

☐ I included one or more examples.

☐ I introduced one example with *For example* and a comma (,).

☐ Every sentence starts with a capital letter and ends with a period.

**B** Exchange paragraphs with a partner. Read and comment on your partner's work.

1. Point out two examples that support the main idea.

*Your sentence, "When I'm…" supports your main idea well.*

*Your sentence about…explains why you …*

2. Give feedback on the paragraph. Check your understanding.

*I'm not sure I understand this sentence. I think you need _____ here.*

**C** Use the checklist and your partner's feedback to revise your writing.

### ▶▶TEST YOURSELF

Complete the following sentences. Share your responses with your teacher.

1. After this writing lesson, I can…

2. I need more help with…

# **1** Use action verbs in the present

**A** Read the conversation. Answer the questions below.

> **Hua:** Hi, Marco. How's that creative sister of yours?
>
> **Marco:** Gina? She's great! She's working on a new painting in her studio right now. She's getting ready for an art show next month.
>
> **Hua:** Incredible! She paints, she writes songs, and she plays all those instruments!
>
> **Marco:** I know. I love her music.

1. Who is Gina?

2. What is Gina doing right now? Where is she?

3. Do we know when Gina writes songs?

4. Do we know how often she plays music?

**B** Study the charts. Circle the three simple present action verbs and underline the two present continuous action verbs in 1A.

| Simple present | Present continuous |
|---|---|
| She often works on paintings on weekends. | She is working on a painting right now. |
| She doesn't watch TV. | She isn't watching TV now. |
| We sometimes write poetry. | We are writing poetry now. |
| They don't play music together very often. | They aren't playing music together now. |

**C** Look at your answers to the questions in 1A. Complete the statements below.

> **Language connection:** Simple present and present continuous action verbs
>
> Most verbs describe actions. These verbs are called _____ verbs. Most
>   (action/stative)
> _____ verbs can be used in the present continuous. Stative verbs are not
>   (action/stative)
> usually used in the _____ .
>   (simple present/present continuous)

**D** Complete the sentences with the simple present or the present continuous form of the verbs in parentheses.

1. Pedro Santana ____works____ at a community college in the math department. (work)

2. In his free time, he _____ math books for school children. (write)

3. Today is Saturday, and Pedro _____ at the college now. (not work)

4. His children _____ Pedro paint today. (help)

## 2 Learn stative verbs in the simple present

**A** Study the chart. Circle the correct words in the sentences below.

| Stative verbs | More stative verbs | | | GRAMMAR NOTE |
|---|---|---|---|---|
| Ari **likes** books about science and travel. | believe | need | smell | • We use stative (non-action) verbs to describe feelings, knowledge, beliefs, and the senses. |
| He **knows** a lot about the outdoors. | dislike | own | sound | • These verbs are usually not used in the present continuous: *He knows a lot.* |
| Ari **thinks** everyone should spend time outdoors. | forget | possess | understand | |
| He **sees** a lot of different things on his travels. | hate | remember | want | |
| Ari **has** a website with pictures from his trips. | hear | seem | love | * *He is knowing a lot.* (incorrect) |
| He **is** a good photographer. | taste | | | |

1. I really ( love / am loving ) to study history.

2. I ( watch / am watching ) TV shows about history every Saturday.

3. I also ( like / am liking ) to read.

4. Right now I ( read / am reading ) an interesting book about U.S. history.

5. I ( know / am knowing ) a lot about history.

6. I ( think / am thinking ) everyone should learn about the past.

**B** Complete the conversation with the words in the box. Then practice the conversation with a partner.

| think | ~~remember~~ | seem | have | know | don't understand |
|---|---|---|---|---|---|

A: Do you __remember__ the page number for our homework assignment?

B: Yes, it's page 23.

A: Thanks. Hey, these questions _____ really easy.

B: Great! By the way, does this book _____ an answer key?

A: I don't _____ . OK, let's get started.

B: Uh-oh. I _____ question one. Do you?

A: No. I don't. I _____ this assignment is going to take all day!

**C** Work in a team. Edit the sentences. Write the corrected sentence.

1. I am not owning a car. __I don't own a car.__

2. This answer isn't seeming right. Can you take a look?

3. Are you understanding information better when you read it or when you hear it?

4. I am thinking that most people are believing that if they work hard, they can reach their goals.

# 3 Listen for action and stative verbs

🔊
1-05
Listen to the speakers. Check (✓) *Action* or *Stative*.

|  | Action | Stative |
|---|---|---|
| 1. |  | ✓ |
| 2. |  |  |
| 3. |  |  |
| 4. |  |  |
| 5. |  |  |
| 6. |  |  |

# 4 Use action and stative verbs to express your opinions

**A** Think about your answers to these questions.

1. How do you remember new words? Name two different ways.

2. Do you think that English is an easy language?

3. How do you feel when you speak English?

4. What do you like/dislike about English?

5. What are three skills that you usually work on in your English class?

6. Which of these skills are you working on today?

**B** Work with a partner. Complete these questions.

1. Do you like learning _____ ?    2. What are you planning to _____ ?

**C** Work in a team. Ask and answer the questions in 4A and 4B. Give as much information as possible. Create a chart with the information.

Mina:  *How do you remember new words?*

Jack:  *I write them in my notebook and review them the next day. What about you?*

Mina:  *I put them on flashcards and test myself on them later.*

| Partners | New words |  |  |  |  |
|---|---|---|---|---|---|
| Jack | notebook |  |  |  |  |
| Mina | flashcards |  |  |  |  |

## ▶▶ TEST YOURSELF

Refer to your chart and write six sentences. Use simple present and present continuous verbs. Use at least three stative verbs.

*Mina makes flashcards to remember new words.*

# **1** Learn ways to express opinions about education

**A** Listen to the conversations. What two subjects are they talking about?
1-06

**B** Listen again for the answers. Compare answers with your partner.
1-06

1. Do the man and woman agree on how many students should be in a class? What is the man's opinion? What is the woman's opinion?

2. Do they agree about the best way to learn English? What is the man's opinion? What is the woman's opinion?

**C** Listen. Write the words the man and woman use to disagree.
1-06

1. _____ , but in a large class you can meet lots of people.

2. _____ . I think talking and listening to people is better.

3. Well, I just listen, of course. _____ , _____ I still think watching TV helps.

# **2** Practice your pronunciation

**A** Listen to the pronunciation of the *t* sounds in these sentences.
1-07

| | |
|---|---|
| I think they're better for students. | The *tt* in *better* is pronounced /d/. |
| They just talk to students all day. | The *t* in *talk* is pronounced /t/. |
| I just listen. | The *t* in *listen* is not pronounced. |
| There's real communication. | The *t* in *communication* is pronounced /sh/. |

**B** Work with a partner. How do you think the *t* is pronounced in these words? Write *d*, *t*, *sh*, or *NP* (not pronounced).

___t___ 1. study      _____ 3. after      _____ 5. little

_____ 2. teacher      _____ 4. education      _____ 6. mortgage

**C** Listen and check. Repeat the words in 2B with a partner.
1-08

## 3 Review *yes/no*, information, and *or* questions

Study the charts. Match the questions with the answers. Work with a partner.
Ask and answer.

| *Yes/No* questions and short answers | |
|---|---|
| **A:** Do you agree? <br> **B:** Yes, I do. | **A:** Does watching TV help you learn? <br> **B:** No, it doesn't. |
| **Or questions** | |
| **A:** Does he like to learn from books or TV? <br> **B:** He likes to learn from books. | **A:** Do they agree or disagree? <br> **B:** They agree. |
| **Information questions** | |
| **A:** Why do you think so? <br> **B:** Because I heard it on the radio. | **A:** Who agrees with you? <br> **B:** Everyone agrees with me! |

___*b*___ 1. When do you study?

_____ 2. Do you need a quiet place to study?

_____ 3. Do you like or dislike the Internet?

_____ 4. What does *visual* mean?

a. Yes, I do.

b. After my children are asleep.

c. It means *connected with seeing*.

d. I like it, but I don't use it often.

## 4 Building conversation skills

**A** Look at the picture and the conversation in 4B. What is the purpose of the conversation? How do you know?

 **B** Listen to the sample conversation. What do they disagree on?

1-09

**A:** Do you think teachers should get more money?

**B:** I don't know. Maybe, but their job seems easy.

**A:** Easy? Really? Why do you say that?

**B:** Well, they just talk to students all day. That's not very difficult.

**A:** I'm not sure I agree. I think it looks like hard work.

### IN OTHER WORDS...

Disagreeing politely

*I'm not sure I agree.*
*You have a point, but…*
*Maybe you're right, but…*
*That's true, but…*

**C** Role-play the situation below.

| Talk about | Roles | Instructions | Remember |
|---|---|---|---|
| Comparing opinions on appropriate classroom behavior | Classmate 1 | You think using teachers' first names is rude. | Use key phrases from 4B <br> Disagree politely |
| | Classmate 2 | You think it's OK to use teachers' first names. | |

## 5 Focus on listening for details

**A** Do you agree or disagree with the statement below? Why or why not? Discuss your opinion with a partner and state your reasons.

*The public schools in our area are doing an excellent job.*

**B** Prepare to listen. Read the sentences.

1. Mr. Fred Holt is from Hills County _____ .

2. Right now, there are _____ students in most classes.

3. We just need a small _____ in state taxes.

4. We hope to install _____ in every high school next year.

5. I agree that we need _____ , but safety is important too.

**C** Listen. Complete the sentences in 5B. Compare your answers with a partner.

1-10

## 6 Discuss

**A** Work with a group. Read the question and collaborate to make a chart.
*What kinds of job skills can you learn from these classroom activities: working with a partner, taking notes, group discussions, role play, and learning new vocabulary?*

A: *In my opinion, taking notes is a skill you can use at work.*

B: *I would agree, especially if you are a visual learner.*

C: *Maybe, but I think just listening carefully is more important.*

**B** Report the results of your discussion to the class.

*We think that role play can help you practice appropriate ways to interact with other people at work.*

> **SPEAKING NOTE**
>
> **Expressing an opinion/agreeing and disagreeing**
> *In my opinion,…*
> *I would agree.*
> *I have to disagree.*
> *To me, …*
> *I couldn't agree more!*
> *Maybe, but I think….*

---

## ▶ TEST YOURSELF

Assess your participation in the group and class discussions. Today I was able to…

☐ listen effectively     ☐ disagree politely

☐ speak accurately     ☐ ask questions

# 1 Read

### A Talk about the questions with your classmates.

1. Do you worry about taking tests? Why or why not?
2. What advice would you give a friend who is worried about a test?

### B Read the definitions.

college entrance exam: (n) a test students take to get into a college or university

concentrate: (v) to give all your attention to something

manageable: (adj) not too big or difficult to control

### C Preview the reading. Look at the title, the subheadings in red, and the bullets. What do you think the writer is going to talk about? Circle the answer.

a. Types of tests and types of test anxiety

b. The definition of test anxiety and possible solutions.

### D Read the article. What is test anxiety?

### It's Not Just for Students!

> **READER'S NOTE**
> Bullets, or bullet points, help the writer list examples and help the reader find information.

How do you feel when you have to take a test? Does a driving test, a test you take when you apply for a job, the GED® test, or a college entrance exam make you
5 nervous? Tests are a part of life, and for many people, test anxiety is too.

**What is test anxiety?**
It's normal to feel nervous before or during a test. In fact, feeling a little
10 stressed can help you focus and can even help you do well. However, if stress is so strong that it's difficult to study for or take a test, then test anxiety is a problem. Some people develop physical symptoms
15 such as headaches and nausea. Other symptoms of test anxiety are emotional, such as feeling angry or afraid. If you find that you are focusing more on anxiety than on preparing for a test, then test anxiety
20 can really interfere with success.

**What can you do?**
Experts recommend using these strategies[1] to deal with test anxiety:
• **Take good care of yourself.** Make sure you
25 are getting enough sleep and exercise.
• **During an exam, quick breaks can help you focus.** Look at something else in the room for a moment or two, and then go back to the test.
• **Visualize success.** Think about how you will
30 feel when you do well on the test. Thinking positively can really help.
• **If you feel nervous during the test, try to relax.** Take deep breaths; breathing slowly and breathing in plenty of air can really help.
35 • **Reward yourself after the test.** Have a nice lunch or meet friends for a movie. You did it!

The next time you have to take a test, follow the experts' suggestions. You'll see: they help!

[1]strategies: plans you make to help you reach a goal
*Source: Penn State Learning*

### E Read the article again. Is the writer trying to encourage or discourage people who have test anxiety? Underline phrases that support your answer.

**F** Choose the correct answer(s). More than one answer is possible. For each answer, write the line number(s) where you found the answer.

1. Someone with test anxiety might feel _____ . _____
   ⓐ angry
   ⓑ adventurous
   ⓒ nauseous

2. Test anxiety is a problem when we focus on the anxiety, and not on _____ . _____
   ⓐ our emotions
   ⓑ what we are doing
   ⓒ physical symptoms

3. Experts believe that _____ . _____
   ⓐ feeling angry can help you focus
   ⓑ most people have test anxiety
   ⓒ strategies can help you manage anxiety

4. Visualizing success means thinking about _____ . _____
   ⓐ how you felt before the test
   ⓑ how you feel during the test
   ⓒ how you want to feel after the test

# 2 Word study

**A** Study the chart. Complete the sentences below. Use a dictionary for words you don't know.

| The suffix *-ize* | | | |
| --- | --- | --- | --- |
| The suffix *-ize* means to cause something to become something. | | | |
| visualize | I try to **visualize** how good I will feel after a test; it reduces my test anxiety. | | |
| strategize | Our group got together to **strategize** the best way to study for our big test. | | |
| maximize | minimize | equalize | characterize |
| dramatize | immobilize | emphasize | standardize |

1. How would you _characterize_ yourself—are you usually relaxed or anxious before a test?
2. Experts _____ the importance of rest before a big exam.
3. Don't let stress _____ you, or make you feel that there is nothing you can do.
4. If you want to _____ test anxiety, try to _____ your positive thinking!

**B** Write a sentence about each topic. Use the underlined word in your sentence.

1. something you like to <u>visualize</u> when you are nervous or worried

_____

2. ways to <u>minimize</u> anxiety

_____

3. a <u>standardized</u> test you have taken or expect to take

_____

# 3 Talk it over

## A Look at the graph and read the note. Complete the sentences and answer the questions.

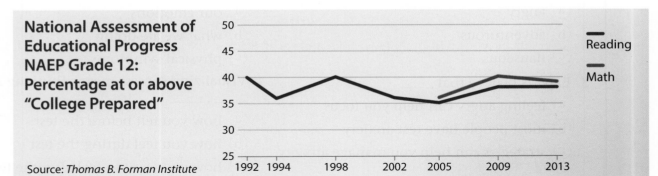

National Assessment of Educational Progress NAEP Grade 12: Percentage at or above "College Prepared"

Source: *Thomas B. Forman Institute*

Reading

Math

The U.S. Department of Education's National Assessment of Educational Progress (NAEP) tracks data on what America's students know and can do in a variety of subject areas, including math, reading, science, the arts, and more. The NAEP uses this data to report on how many students are "college-ready." From 1992 to 2013, the number of recent high school graduates who enrolled in college rose from 61 percent to 66 percent. In the same time period, the college preparedness rate in reading dropped from 40 percent to 38 percent. So, while more students are starting college, they are less prepared for college than in the past.

**READER'S NOTE**
Reading complex charts and texts several times can help in understanding them. Read first for the main idea, then for details, and then again to work on new vocabulary words.

Source: NAEP

1. In 2013, __38__ percent of 12th grade students were college-ready in reading.

2. _____ was the lowest year. _____ percent of 12th grade students were college-ready in reading.

3. The graph shows the percentage of students who were _____ over a time period of _____ years.

4. The note includes data on the number of students who _____ .

5. What data do both the chart and the note include? _____

## B Work with a partner to answer the questions.

1. How would you define "college-ready"? Why?

2. Why do you think the percentage of students who are "college-ready" when they leave high school is dropping?

3. What should colleges do to help new students get ready?

4. Should high schools be responsible for making more of their students college-ready?

---

 BRING IT TO LIFE

Use the library or the Internet to research how colleges in your area test new students for placement in classes. Is the system fair? Talk with your classmates.

**A** Listen to the employees. What are they talking about?

🔊 1-11

**B** Listen to the employees again. Then write *T* next to the true statements.

🔊 1-11

_____ 1. Employees will be able to take a class at work.

_____ 2. Employees will have to pay for the classes.

_____ 3. The classes will be half during work and half after work.

_____ 4. Employees will have to take a test before they start the class.

🔊 1-11

**C** Listen again. What two things did one employee not understand?

**D** Read the chart. Discuss the questions below with your class.

| When you don't understand something you can | |
| --- | --- |
| **Do this** <br> • Raise your hand to ask a question <br> • Raise one hand and draw in your breath <br> • Point to the word or thing you don't understand and raise your eyebrows | **Say this** <br> I don't understand. <br> Could you help me with this? I'm lost. <br> Wait…I'm lost. <br> I'm having trouble understanding. <br> Could you explain? |

1. Why is it important to let someone know when you don't understand?

2. What else can you do with your hands or face to show that you don't understand?

3. In a formal situation, what should you not say when you don't understand?

**E** Work with a partner. Ask for help with the words in bold.

| Information | Question |
| --- | --- |
| There's a **notice** in the staff room. | *I don't understand. What's a notice?* |
| The **placement test** is **tomorrow**. | |
| The classes are on **release time**. | |

**F** Have a conversation at work.

1. Work with a group to brainstorm three ideas your company has to help employees.

2. Take turns telling each other about the opportunities your company is offering, and asking for help to understand. Use the ideas from your list and from this page.

**A:** *Did you see the memo in the lunch room? It says…*

**B:** *That sounds interesting.*

**C:** *Wait… I'm lost. What…*

**A** Collaborate to write 10 questions about the picture. Select one word or phrase from the word box for each question.

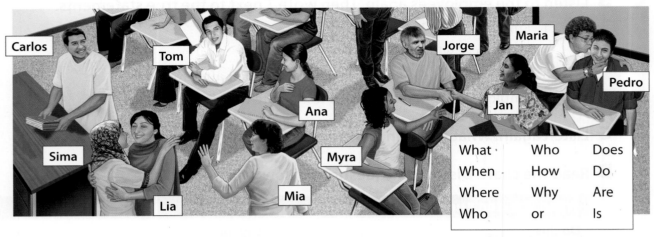

**B** Name the people having each conversation. Explain your choices to your team.

Who says it?

_____ : *Do you want to go out tonight?*

_____ : *Sorry, tonight I just want to spend time at home.*

_____ : *You two seem like you need an introduction.*

_____ : *Not really. Jorge and I know each other from last semester.*

_____ : *Hi! Did you get my books for me?*

_____ : *Yes, I have them right here.*

_____ : *You're back! Why do you always miss class?*

_____ : *I love this class, but my shift changes every week.*

_____ : *It's good to see you! How's your family?*

_____ : *Everyone's well, I'm happy to say.*

**C** Circle the stative verbs and underline the action verbs in the conversation. Compare your choices to your teammates' choices.

**D** Collaborate to complete the conversation between four friends. Use the simple present or present continuous and your own ideas. Then act it out.

**A:** I _____ that someday I would like to be a _____ .
            (think)                                              (name of occupation)

**B:** That _____ interesting.  I _____ _____ about that career.
           (sound)                            (know)         (a little/a lot)

**C:** They _____ a job fair in the auditorium right now.  Let's go!
             (hold)

**D:** I can't, sorry. I _____ the 2:00 bus.
                 (catch)

**A:** I'm sorry to tell you this, but your bus _____ away right now.
                                              (drive)

## E Work in a team. Follow the steps below to complete the task.

1. Assign team roles: manager, director, editor, actors.

2. Choose a person from the list on the right.

3. Write a list of strategies for this person. Use a main idea and bullets.

4. Read your suggestions to the class.

**People**
- a kinesthetic learner who has trouble studying
- a person who becomes really nervous before a test
- a quiet person who doesn't like to talk in class
- a person who has trouble prioritizing things he or she needs to do to reach a goal
- a social person who hates studying alone

## F Interview three classmates. Write their answers.

1. What are three words from this unit that describe you?

2. What is one word from this unit that doesn't describe you?

3. Do you think you are mostly a visual, an auditory, or a kinesthetic learner?

4. What is the best way for you to study? Why?

5. In your opinion, what's the best way to control test anxiety?

## G Report your results for Exercise F, #3 to the class. Make a pie chart with your class results.

# PROBLEM SOLVING

1-12

## A Listen and read about Rita.

Rita lives with two roommates. They're all good friends. Rita works part-time and goes to school. Her roommates aren't students; they work. Rita's classes are challenging, and she often has a lot of homework. She studies best when the apartment is quiet. But when her roommates come home from work, they don't want to be quiet. They want to enjoy the evening. When they talk and play music, Rita can't concentrate. She doesn't know what to do.

## B Work with your classmates. Respond to the prompts.

1. Identify Rita's problem.

2. Brainstorm solutions Rita could try. What are some things she could say? What should she *not* say?

UNIT

# 2 Breaking News

**A LOOK AT**
- News and current events
- The past passive
- Expressing an opinion

## LESSON 1 VOCABULARY

## 1 Identify news sources

### A Collaborate with your classmates. Answer the questions about the web page.

1. What kind of news or information can you get from each part of the website?
2. Which part of a news website would you look at first? Why?

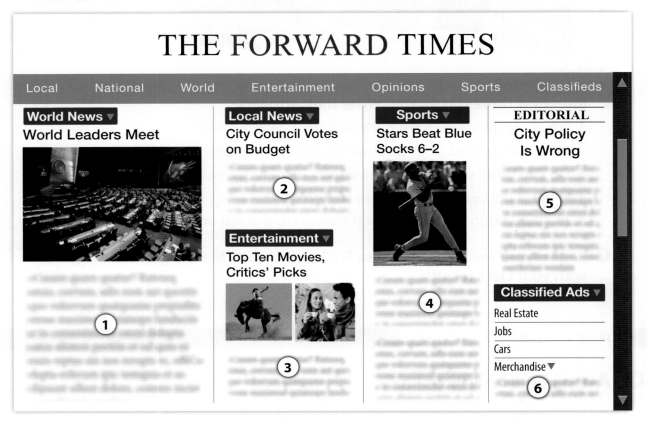

THE FORWARD TIMES

| Local | National | World | Entertainment | Opinions | Sports | Classifieds |

**World News ▾**
World Leaders Meet

**Local News ▾**
City Council Votes on Budget

**Entertainment ▾**
Top Ten Movies, Critics' Picks

**Sports ▾**
Stars Beat Blue Socks 6–2

**EDITORIAL**
City Policy Is Wrong

**Classified Ads ▾**
Real Estate
Jobs
Cars
Merchandise ▾

### B Write the number from the parts of the website in front of each question. Then listen and check your work.

🔊 1-13

__5__ 1. Where can you read opinions about the news?

____ 2. Where can you look for a job, or advertise something you want to sell?

____ 3. For news about other countries, what should you read?

____ 4. Where can you get information about baseball, football and soccer?

____ 5. To see news about your city and your neighborhood, what should you read?

____ 6. What page would you look at for information about movies and music?

### C Listen again. What news source does Wanda like? What news sources does Stan like?

🔊 1-13

## 2 Learn more types of news

**A** Look at the news website. Match the news vocabulary with the definitions.

___e___ 1. top story

_____ 2. traffic report

_____ 3. current events

_____ 4. weather forecast

_____ 5. headlines

a. information about highway conditions

b. information on what to expect outside

c. news stories that have happened recently

d. one sentence about each important news story

e. the most important or most recent news event

**B** Work with a partner. Practice the conversation. Use the words in 2A.

A: *What news source do you go to for the top story?*

B: *I usually listen to the news on the radio on my way to work.*

**C** Survey your classmates in order to report on the questions below.

1. What kind of news is most important to you? Why?

2. What source(s) do you like to use to get the news? Why?

3. What kind of news do you never read or listen to? Why?

**D** Report the results of your research.

*Our team discovered that most of our classmates consider _____ news the most important. Some of the reasons are …*

*Most of our classmates like to get the news from …*

---

## ▶▶ TEST YOURSELF

Work with a partner. Take turns reading and responding to the prompts in 1B.

**Partner A:** Read prompts 1–3. Partner B: Listen and write the vocabulary words.
**Partner B:** Read prompts 4–6. Partner A: Listen and write the vocabulary words.

# 1 Prepare to write

### A Look at the picture. Talk about the questions with your class.

1. What happened on this street?

2. How do you think the neighbors feel?

### B Listen and read the news story.
1-14

**WRITER'S NOTE**

Use adverbial time clauses to establish a sequence of events in the past.

*When/as soon as the neighbors saw the graffiti, they called the police.*

*Mr. Suk didn't hear about the graffiti until he read the news the next day.*

## Police Called in Lakeland

**Tuesday, November 8**

A group of teenagers painted graffiti on an empty building in Lakeland last night. When angry neighbors saw them, they called the police. The police responded to the call, and the teens were taken to the Lakeland Police Station.

Neighbors disagree about the graffiti. Some people don't like it. They say that it is changing the way the neighborhood looks and not for the better. However, the building's owner, Mr. Anwar Suk, doesn't mind the graffiti. He says that it is neighborhood art.

Next week, the chief of police will hold a community meeting to talk about the neighborhood disagreement. The chief is expecting a big turnout among community members.

### C Study the news story. Answer the questions.

1. Paragraph 1: How did the neighbors react when they saw the graffiti?

_____

2. Paragraph 2: How is Mr. Suk's opinion different from the angry neighbors' opinion?

_____

3. Paragraph 3: Who will probably attend the community meeting next week?

_____

## 2 Plan and write

**A Talk about the questions with your class. Take notes.**

1. Name three or four recent local, national, or international events.

2. Choose one event. What happened?

**B Write a news story about a recent event in your community. Use the model news story in 1B and the questions below to help you.**

Paragraph 1: What happened?
<br>When and where did it happen?
<br>Who was involved?

Paragraph 2: How did people react to the event?

Paragraph 3: What will happen next?

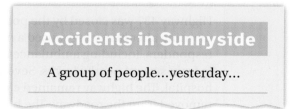

**Accidents in Sunnyside**

A group of people...yesterday...

## 3 Get feedback and revise

**A Use the editing checklist to review your writing. Check (✔) the true sentences.**

☐ My news story tells about an event that happened recently.

☐ It answers the questions *who, what, when, where,* and *how.*

☐ My story has three paragraphs.

☐ The first line of each paragraph is indented.

☐ My story focuses on facts and not on opinions.

**B Exchange news stories with a partner. Read and comment on your partner's work.**

1. Point out the sentences that you think are well written.

   *Your sentence, "As soon as ...." makes the sequence of events clear.*

   *You answered all of the* who, what, where, why, when *questions.*

2. Give feedback about the story. Check your understanding.

   *I'm not sure I understand the order of events here.*

   *I think you need a _____ here.*

**C Use the checklist and your partner's feedback to revise your writing.**

---

## ▸▸ TEST YOURSELF

Write a different news story about another interesting event at your workplace, in your neighborhood, or at your school.

## 1 Use the past passive

**A** Read the news article. Answer the questions below.

| Local | National | World | Entertainment | Opinions | Sports | Classifieds |
|---|---|---|---|---|---|---|

### Highway 437 Closed in Multi-Car Accident by Min Pham

Highway 437 was closed by the police for six hours early yesterday morning after heavy fog caused a multi-car accident. Emergency responders, including ambulances and several fire trucks, were called in from several nearby towns. Several injured people were taken to the hospital. The highway remained closed until the damaged cars were removed from the roadway. The highway was reopened just before noon.

1. Who closed Highway 437 yesterday morning?

2. Do we know who called in the emergency responders?

3. Who do you think took the injured people to the hospital?

4. Do we know who reopened the road? Is it important to know?

**B** Study the chart. Underline 5 past passive verbs in the article in 1A.

| The Past Passive | | |
|---|---|---|
| **Subject** | ***was/were* + past participle** | |
| An accident | was caused | by the fog last night. |
| Min | wasn't taken | to the hospital by the paramedics. |
| Several people | were taken | to the hospital after the accident. |
| The cars | weren't removed | for two hours because of the fog. |

**C** Look at your answers to the questions in 1A. Complete the statements below.

**Language connection:** Using the past passive

We usually use the active voice to say what people or things do or did. We can use the passive voice in these situations:

- when an action is _____ important than the person or thing who did it
  (more/less)
- when we don't _____ who or what performed the action
  (know/question)
- when we don't want to _____ who performed the action, or
  (know/say)
- when it's already _____ who performed the action.
  (clear/significant)

**D** **Complete the sentences with the past passive. Use the verbs in parentheses.**

1. The accident _was caused_ by the heavy fog. (cause)
2. Two drivers _____ in the crash. (injure)
3. As soon as the road was clear, it _____ . (reopen)
4. The article _____ after the accident. (write)
5. The photos _____ by a local news photographer. (take)

**E** **Work with your team. Rewrite the sentences in the past passive. Use *by* + noun to say who or what performed the action.**

1. After the accident, the police closed Highway 437.
   _After the accident, Highway 437 was closed by the police._
2. Paramedics took the injured people to the hospital.
   _____
3. Several tow trucks removed the cars from the highway.
   _____
4. Traffic reporters in a helicopter took the photos we saw on the news.
   _____

## 2 Use past passive questions

**A** **Study the charts.**

| Past Passive Questions | |
| --- | --- |
| **Yes/No questions** | **Information questions** |
| A: Was the highway reopened?<br>B: Yes, it was. | A: When was the highway reopened?<br>B: It was reopened an hour after the accident. |
| A: Were people taken to the hospital?<br>B: Yes, they were. | A: Where were the injured people taken?<br>B: They were taken to City Hospital. |

**B** **Complete the conversation with the past passive of the verbs in parentheses.**

A: There was a big accident on the highway this morning.

B: Really? What caused the accident?

A: It _was caused_ by two deer. (cause) They ran across the road.

B: _____ anyone _____ ? (hit)

A: No. Thankfully no one _____ . (hit)

B: What about the deer? _____ they _____ ? (hurt)

A: One deer _____ (hit). It _____ . (not hurt)

## 3 Listen for the past passive to determine the meaning

🔊
1-15

**Listen to the conversations. Check (✔) the correct statement.**

1. _____ a. Our car hit a tree.

   _✓_ b. A tree hit our car.

2. _____ a. The neighbors gave the information to the reporter.

   _____ b. The reporter gave the information to the neighbors.

3. _____ a. The teenagers' parents called the police.

   _____ b. The police called the teenagers' parents.

4. _____ a. A fire caused an electrical problem.

   _____ b. An electrical problem caused the fire.

## 4 Use the past passive to talk about real events

**A** **Use the past passive to write headlines for two recent news stories. Use the questions for ideas.**

What was built / damaged / closed / discovered?

Who was rescued / arrested / honored / welcomed home?

**B** **Work with a partner. Write two more news headlines. Write about real news stories, or create a story of your own.**

1. _____

2. _____

**C** **Work in a team. Ask and answer questions about the headlines you wrote in 4A and 4B. Give more information. Create a chart with notes about each story.**

**Brenda:** *Tell me more about the big storm. How much of the city was flooded?*

**Lian:** *The whole downtown was flooded. A lot of buildings were damaged.*

| Reporter | Story | Story notes |
|---|---|---|
| Lian | Big rainstorm | Downtown was flooded<br>Buildings were damaged |
|  |  |  |

## ▶▶ TEST YOURSELF

Close your book. Refer to your chart and write five sentences about your classmates' news stories. Use the past passive.

# 1 Learn ways to talk about a current event

🔊 1-16 **A** Listen to the conversation. What did the city want?

*to make a long story short = to tell the most important fact

🔊 1-16 **B** Listen again for the answers. Compare answers with your partner.

1. What did the protesters want?
2. What happened to traffic downtown during the protest?
3. How do the speakers feel about food trucks? Why?

🔊 1-16 **C** Listen. Write the words the speakers use to express agreement.

1. The protesters were really upset. _____ !
2. _____ . It's important to support local businesses.

# 2 Practice your pronunciation

🔊 1-17 **A** Listen to the ways the speakers use stress to clarify their meaning in the conversation. Underline the words that are stressed.

A: The city wanted to prohibit food trucks.

B: Limit food trucks?

A: No, not limit food trucks, prohibit food trucks.

**B** Work with a partner. Underline the words you think are stressed.

1. A: The tree wasn't cut down.
   B: It was cut down?
   A: No, it wasn't cut down.

2. A: The protesters were really upset.
   B: The police were upset?
   A: No, the protesters.

🔊 1-18 **C** Listen and check. Then practice the conversations in 2A and 2B with a partner.

## 3 Learn reflexive pronouns

**A** Study the chart. Underline the endings of the reflexive pronouns.

| Subject pronouns | Reflexive pronouns |
|---|---|
| I | myself |
| you | yourself |
| he | himself |
| she | herself |
| it | itself |
| we | ourselves |
| you | yourselves |
| they | themselves |

**GRAMMAR NOTE**

- Reflexive pronouns are used when the subject and object of the sentence refer to the same people or things.
  *I hurt myself.   He gave himself a raise.*
- Use *by* + reflexive pronoun to say that someone or something is alone or does something without help.
  *She went by herself.* = She went alone.

**B** Check your understanding. Complete the sentences with reflexive pronouns.

1. Did you see the protest _yourself_ or did you see it on the news?

2. We were watching the news, and we saw _____ on TV!

3. Did you and Paul go by _____ , or did Tim go with you?

4. She was surprised to see a picture of _____ on a news website.

## 4 Building conversation skills

**A** Look at the picture and the conversation in 4B. What is the purpose of the conversation? How do you know?

**B** Listen to the sample conversation. How does Dani's opinion compare to the neighbors' opinion about the trees?

1-19

A: Dani, did you see the news? The city is planning to cut down a lot of old trees in our neighborhood. The neighbors are really upset.

B: I can understand that. What did the mayor say?

A: She said that the trees have been damaged by disease or insects, and that that's why they have to be cut down.

B: That's really too bad. Do you think the city will replace them?

A: I hope so. If not, maybe we could replace some of them ourselves.

B: I agree. That's a great idea, Alex.

"Communities upset by tree-removal plan…"

**IN OTHER WORDS...**

Expressing agreement
*I can understand that.*
*I agree.*
*That makes sense to me.*
*I'd agree with that.*

**C** Role-play the situation below.

| Talk about | Roles | Instructions | Remember |
|---|---|---|---|
| Discussing local news | Friend 1 | The city council is closing your community center. People are upset. Volunteer to help repair the center. | Use key phrases from 4B |
| | Friend 2 | You understand the people who are upset. Maybe the building could be repaired. | Express agreement |

# 5 Focus on listening for details

**A** Do you agree or disagree with the statement below? Why or why not? Discuss your opinion with a partner and state your reasons.

*Reporting the news can be a dangerous job.*

**B** Prepare to listen. Read the sentences. In the right column, predict the missing word or words you will hear in the news report.

| Vocabulary | Prediction |
|---|---|
| 1. A _____ is expected to reach Florida on Wednesday. | |
| 2. Local residents were told to _____ by noon today. | |
| 3. Residents will be able to stay in local _____ . | |
| 4. Local aid agencies are bringing in _____ for residents. | |
| 5. News reporters were also _____ the area. | |

🔊 1-20 **C** Listen. Complete the sentences in 5B. Compare your answers with a partner.

# 6 Discuss

**A** Work with a group. Rate each job from very safe (1) to very dangerous (5). State your reasons.

- Reporters
- Emergency responders
- Police officers

A: *I think reporters' jobs are among the most dangerous.*
B: *Do you mean all reporters?*

**B** Report the results of your discussion to the class.

*We think that…jobs are the most dangerous because …*

> **SPEAKING NOTE**
>
> **Questioning and restating to check understanding**
> *Do you mean ….?*
> *Let me be sure I understand.*
> *Are you saying…?*
> *Did I understand you correctly?*
> *Is this….?*

---

## ▶▶ TEST YOURSELF

Assess your participation in the group and class discussions. Today I was able to…

☐ listen effectively      ☐ check understanding

☐ speak accurately      ☐ ask questions

# 1 Read

## A Talk about the questions with your classmates.

1. Which news source do you use most: TV, radio, online news sites, newspapers, or magazines? Why?
2. What two sources are people most likely to use to get local news?

## B Read the definitions.

figure: (n) a number

rely on: (v) count on; have confidence in

survey: (n) a set of questions used to get an idea of people's opinions

## C Preview the reading. Scan the article and look for numbers. What is the article about? Circle the answer.

a. The number of people who pay attention to the news

b. How people responded to a survey in 2014

c. The number of people who read the news in 2014

## D Read the article. What two ways did the survey divide people?

### Americans and the News

Where do you get the news? Many of us rely on traditional sources, like TV or a newspaper. Others like online news, or social media. But what do we really
5 know about people's news habits?

In a recent survey, people were asked about the news sources they prefer, and about the devices they use to get the news. The results may surprise you.
10 Many people believe that age makes a big difference in how people get the news. In reality, a 2014 survey of 1,492 adults found that the majority of Americans across generations now
15 combine sources and technologies to get their news. In fact, the average American uses four different devices or technologies, and four or five sources, for news.

The source may also depend on the
20 kind of news. People reported that they are most likely to use newspapers for local news, and cable TV for news on politics, international news, and social issues. They rely on local TV for weather, traffic, crime
25 and health news.

Younger adults are more likely to use social media for news, but all age groups reported using it. Interestingly, while 43 percent said they trust news that comes
30 directly from a news organization, that figure is only 15 percent for news on social media. Gender makes a difference too. Women are more likely to use social media, while men are more likely to watch
35 cable news.

Technology may change, but one thing stays the same: people want to know what's going on.

Source: *American Press Institute*

**E** Read the article again. Does the writer express an opinion about the information in the article? Explain your answer.

**F** Answer the questions. For each answer, write the line number(s) where you found the answer.

1. What was the survey about? _____

_____

2. What are the two most-used sources to get the news? _____

_____

3. Who is most likely to use social media to get news? _____

_____

4. What do the majority of people think about the reliability of news on social media? _____

_____

# 2 Word study

**A** Study the chart. Complete the sentences below. Use a dictionary for words that are not familiar.

| The suffix *-ity* |
| --- |

The suffix *-ity* means *a quality or condition*. Add *-ity* to some adjectives to make a related noun.

real — There has been a **real** increase in people's use of social media to get news.
reality — In **reality**, age doesn't make a difference in people's choice of news sources.

Pronunciation note: There is sometimes a change in word stress when *-ity* is added to an adjective.

| | | | | | |
| --- | --- | --- | --- | --- | --- |
| **a**ctive | **a**ctivity | **ma**jor | ma**jor**ity | **a**ble | a**bi**lity |
| **clear** | **clar**ity | **mo**bile | mo**bi**lity | **sim**ilar | simi**lar**ity |

1. The <u>majority</u> of Americans get their news from more than one source.
2. It's important to have the _____ to evaluate your news source.
3. A good news story can bring _____ to a complicated issue.
4. The survey found a lot of _____ between people of different age groups.
5. New technologies have really increased reporters' _____ .

**B** Write a sentence about each topic. Use the underlined word in your sentence.

1. a <u>similarity</u> between you and someone older than you

_____

2. an <u>activity</u> you enjoy

_____

3. something you would like to have the <u>ability</u> to do

_____

## 3 Talk it over

**A** Read the article. Complete the sentences and answer the questions.

### Citizen Journalism: Pros and Cons

**C**itizen journalism is a term commonly used when ordinary citizens who are not professional journalists write about and publish information about current events 5 as they occur. The rise of citizen journalism has largely been made possible by modern technology, blogs and social media, which allow individuals to post information, opinions, photos, and videos that others 10 all over the world can access.

Some professional journalists say that citizen journalism is unreliable, unprofessional, and biased (focused on opinions rather than facts). They claim that access to a cell phone camera and a social media site are not the equivalent of years of professional training 15 and experience.

Supporters of citizen journalism say that community members may be the best source of information about local communities that could be too small to be covered by traditional news media. They also argue that citizen journalism allows for more diversity of opinions and interests than traditional media.

> **READER'S NOTE**
> Illustrations (charts, graphics, or cartoons) support the writer's point visually, and help the reader understand material in the text.

1. In the 'pro' argument, the writer says that the best source of local information and diverse opinions may be _____ .

2. In the 'con' argument, the writer implies that professional journalists are more likely to report based on facts, while citizen journalists may be more _____ .

3. How does the editorial cartoon align with, or support, the information in the article?

4. Give an example of a situation where citizen journalism has been important.

**B** Work with a partner to discuss the questions.

1. Are citizen journalists important in reporting current events?

2. Is there too much bad news on traditional TV and news websites?

3. Do you think that news reporters sometimes create news?

---

## ⏻ BRING IT TO LIFE

Bring a news story in a newspaper or magazine, or online to class. Discuss how the article answers the questions *who*, *what*, *where*, *when*, and *why*.

**◄))** **A** Listen to the staff meeting. What does the supervisor want to tell the employees?
1-21

**◄))** **B** Listen again. Mark the sentences *T* (true) or *F* (false).
1-21

   __F__ 1. Employees' pay is going to be cut.

   _____ 2. The supervisor will talk to some of the employees herself today.

   _____ 3. The supervisor wants the employees to ask questions.

   _____ 4. The employees don't tell the supervisor their opinions.

   _____ 5. The supervisor is not concerned about good communication.

**◄))** **C** Listen again. What facts did you hear? What opinions were expressed? Tell a partner.
1-21

**D** Read the chart. Discuss the questions below with your class.

| When you want to give your opinion in a group or during a meeting | | |
|---|---|---|
| **Do this**<br>• Raise one hand a little<br>• Hold one hand in front of you<br>• Tilt your head a little to one side<br>• Lean forward | **Say this**<br>In my opinion, …<br>If I can offer an opinion, …<br>I feel that… | Personally, …<br>To my mind, …<br>As far as I'm concerned, …<br>For me, … |

1. Why is it important to be polite when you state your opinion?

2. What else can you do if you disagree with the opinions of the people you are talking to?

3. In a formal situation, what should you not say when you give your opinion?

**E** Work with a partner. Take turns reading the questions and expressing an opinion.

1. Is it important for supervisors to hold staff meetings? Why/why not?

2. Is it easy or difficult to tell a supervisor your opinion? Why?

3. Why is good communication important in the workplace?

**F** Have a staff meeting.

1. Work with a group. List one thing a supervisor wants to tell the staff, and one thing the supervisor wants the staff's opinion on.

2. Choose one person to be the supervisor. Begin the meeting. Use the ideas from your list and from this page.

A: *Thanks for coming, everyone. I want to talk about some changes we need to make in the schedule. We are going to … and… OK, are there any questions?*

B: *Um…When will this happen?*

A: *I would like to get your opinion on how we can improve our ads.*

C: *If I can offer an opinion, …*

# TEAMWORK & LANGUAGE REVIEW

**A** Collaborate to write news headlines about the natural disasters below. Use the model and the past passive form of the verbs.

| damage | destroy | hit | strike |
|---|---|---|---|

forest fire

tsunami

tornado

earthquake

flood

blizzard

At (<u>time</u>), (<u>place</u>) (noun) (<u>past passive</u>) by a (<u>natural disaster</u>) .

*Yesterday, at 6 p.m., in southern California, several parks were destroyed by a forest fire.*

**B** Take turns asking and answering the questions about one of the disasters in A. Use the past passive and *by* + noun.

1. What happened?
2. What did the authorities close?
3. What kind of emergency workers handled the situation?
4. How many people did the emergency workers rescue?
5. When did the officials reopen the area?

**C** Complete the conversation between two married emergency workers. Use reflexive pronouns. Explain your choices.

A: Did you see the kitchen? It's a disaster!

B: Shhh. Don't say that. The kids cooked our anniversary dinner _____ .

A: Well, we're going to need to take _____ out to dinner.

B: Speak for _____ ! I want to see what they prepared.

A: I can see for _____ . It's all over the kitchen!

**D** Act out the conversation with your team.

**E** **Work in a team. Follow the steps below to complete the task.**

1. Assign team roles: news writers, editorial writer and editor.

2. Choose a news story that is important in your community right now. Check the list for ideas.

3. Identify the facts you have about the issue.

4. Discuss your opinions on the issue.

5. Write a news story and a short editorial about the issue.

6. Read your story and editorial to the class.

| Stories |
|---|
| • traffic problems or dangerous streets |
| • weather damage |
| • housing problems |
| • not enough activities for seniors/adults/teens |

**F** **Interview three classmates. Write their answers.**

1. How much time do you spend each week reading or listening to the news?

2. Do you think people have a responsibility to know about current events? Why or why not?

3. In your opinion, what have been the three most important events in the news this year?

**G** **Report your results for Exercise F, #3 to the class. Make a bar graph of your class results.**

## PROBLEM SOLVING

1-22

**A** **Listen and read about Anton.**

> Before Anton came to the United States, he always read the newspaper, watched the news on TV, and followed the international news on the Internet. He loved to talk to his friends about current events.
>
> However, since Anton came to the U.S., getting the news hasn't been so easy. He thinks it is very hard to understand TV and radio news in English. He reads the news online in his own language, but reading it in English is a challenge. At work, his co-workers talk about current events at lunch. Anton would like to be able to talk about his opinion, too.

**B** **Work with your classmates. Respond to the prompts.**

1. Identify Anton's problem.

2. Make a list of strategies Anton could try.

3. What is the best strategy? Why do you think so? What do you think will happen if he chooses that strategy?

UNIT
# 3 Going Places

A LOOK AT
- Travel and transportation
- Reported speech
- Making suggestions

## LESSON 1 VOCABULARY

## 1 Identify vocabulary for travel emergencies

**A** Collaborate with your classmates. Brainstorm ways to travel and what to take with you.

**B** Work with a partner. Look at the pictures. Complete the sentences with the words in the box. Leave a blank if you are not sure.

| | | |
|---|---|---|
| called the auto club | had a breakdown | send a tow truck |
| changed the tire | had a flat tire | turned on the hazard lights |
| get directions | raise the hood | put out safety triangles |

Dalia and Emilio were on their way to visit Emilio's parents when they (1) <u>had a breakdown</u>. They pulled over to get out of traffic, and (2) _____ . Dalia (3) _____ . The agent told them to (4) _____ of the car, and said that he would send help.

Hai and Mia and their sons (5) _____ just as they were leaving for their vacation. They pulled over and Hai got out the spare tire. He (6) _____ while Mia and the boys watched.

On Genet's second day on the job as a city bus driver, her bus broke down. She pulled over, reassured the passengers, and (7) _____ in the road behind the bus. Then she called the bus company office to ask them to (8) _____ . Most of the passengers waited for another bus, but one woman decided to (9) _____ from another passenger and walk.

**C** Listen and check your work.
1-23

**D** Listen again. Write the emergencies and solutions you hear in a chart.
1-23

| Emergency | Solution | Solution | Solution |
|---|---|---|---|
| breakdown | hazard lights | | |
| | | | |
| | | | |

**E** Work in a team. Add other travel emergencies and solutions to your chart in 1D. Then add words you want to learn to your vocabulary notebook.

## 2 Learn vocabulary for travel problems

**A** Look at the pictures. Match the pictures with the sentences.

a. out of gas       b. lost       c. stuck in traffic       d. locked out of the car

___d___ 1. She should call the auto club. She needs a locksmith.

_____ 2. He should walk to a gas station.

_____ 3. She should ask someone for directions, or check a GPS.

_____ 4. He's going to be late. He should call his customer.

**B** Work with a partner. Practice the conversation. Use the words in 2A.

**A:** I can't believe this!

**B:** What's the problem?

**A:** I'm locked out of my car. What should I do?

**B:** You should call the auto club.

**C** Conduct research with a team. Write two more questions about travel problems and emergencies. Survey your classmates in order to report on your questions.

1. How have you or someone you know used a cell phone in a travel emergency?
2. What should drivers always have in a car in case of an emergency?

**D** Report the results of your research.

*Our team discovered that people in our class have used cell phones _____ . We feel that drivers should ...*

---

## ▶ TEST YOURSELF

Work with a partner. Take turns reading and responding to the prompts in 1B.

**Partner A:** Read prompts 1–4. Partner B: Listen and write the vocabulary words.
**Partner B:** Read prompts 5–9. Partner A: Listen and write the vocabulary words.

# **1** Prepare to write

**A** Look at the pictures and read the title of the story. Talk about the questions with your class.

1. Who do you think each person is calling?
2. How do the people feel? Why?

## **B** Listen and read the story.

1-24

> **WRITER'S NOTE**
> To repeat a speaker's words, add a comma (,) and quotation marks (" ").

### Then and Now
#### by Ahmed Bell

When I first came to this country, it was very difficult for me to use the phone. I could understand people in person, but listening to people on the phone was a different story.

I got my first car about three years ago, and I haven't had much trouble with it. But when I first got it, I was on my way to work one day and someone ran into the back of my car at a red light. She wasn't going very fast, and everyone was OK, but both cars were slightly damaged.

Then I called my insurance company. I got an automated menu, instead of a person. I could understand the computer's speech, but I had to call back three times before I understood which number to press on the phone. When I got to talk to a real person, she said, "Can you hold?" and I said, "Hold what?" I didn't know that hold can mean wait.

Now, using the phone is much easier for me. I hope I never have another accident, but if I do, at least I will be able to get the information I need.

## **C** Study the story. Answer the questions.

1. Paragraph 1: What was difficult for Ahmed when he first came to the U.S.?
2. Paragraph 2: What did Ahmed have trouble with when he called the insurance company?
3. Paragraph 3: What did "Can you hold?" mean?
4. Paragraph 4: What has changed for Ahmed in the last three years?

## 2 Plan and write

**A Talk about the questions with your class. Take notes.**

1. How is speaking in English on the phone different from communicating in person?

2. Do you get nervous when you have to use the phone in English? Why or why not?

**B Write a story about your experience communicating by phone. Use the model story in 1B and your answers to the questions in 2A.**

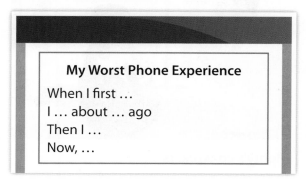

**My Worst Phone Experience**
When I first ...
I ... about ... ago
Then I ...
Now, ...

## 3 Get feedback and revise

**A Use the editing checklist to review your writing. Check (✔) the true sentences.**

☐ I wrote about the past and the present.

☐ I wrote about one of my experiences using the phone.

☐ I used the simple past to write about the past.

☐ I used a comma and quotation marks to repeat a speaker's words.

**B Exchange texts with a partner. Read and comment on your partner's work.**

1. Point out one sentence that you think is interesting.

   *Your sentence, "I could understand ..., but I had to ..." gives a good description of the situation. Your closing paragraph is very clear.*

2. Give feedback about the story. Check your understanding.

   *I'm not sure I understand this sentence.*

   *I think you need to say more about ... here.*

**C Use the checklist and your partner's feedback to revise your writing.**

---

## ▶ TEST YOURSELF

Complete the following sentences. Share your responses with your teacher.

1. After this writing lesson, I can...
2. I need more help with...

## 1 Learn reported speech

### A Look at the pictures. Read the conversation.

I'm stuck in traffic.

Monty

Monty called. He said he was stuck in traffic.

Monty's co-workers

### B Study the charts. Underline the reported speech in 1A.

| Quoted speech | Reported speech | |
|---|---|---|
| Monty said, "I'm stuck in traffic." | He said | (that) he was stuck in traffic. |
| Lia said, "I'm waiting for a tow truck." | She said | (that) she was waiting for a tow truck. |
| They said, "We don't have a GPS." | They said | (that) they didn't have a GPS. |

| GRAMMAR NOTES |
|---|
| Use quoted speech to repeat exactly what someone said.<br>Use reported speech to tell what someone said or wrote. |

### C Complete the statements below.

**Language connection:** Quoted and reported speech

When we want to talk about what someone said, we can use either quoted

speech or reported speech. We use _____ speech when we want to
                                    (quoted/reported)

repeat the speaker's exact words. We use _____ marks around the
                                          (quoted/quotation)

quoted words. We use reported speech to _____ what someone
                                         (repeat/talk about)

said. For quoted speech in the simple present, the reported speech is in the

_____ . For quoted speech in the present continuous, the
(simple present/simple past)

reported speech is in the _____ continuous.
                           (present/past)

**D** Fred invited his friends to dinner, but some of them called because they had problems getting to his home. Complete the sentences with reported speech.

1. Luis said, "I'm lost."

   Luis said that _____ .

2. Alice and Kim said, "We don't know the address."

   Alice and Kim said _____ .

## 2 Learn reported speech with *told* + noun or pronoun

**A** Study the chart. Complete the sentences with *said* or *told*.

| Quoted speech | Reported speech | |
|---|---|---|
| Bob said, "Lee, I have a flat tire." | Bob said<br>Bob told Lee<br>Bob told her | (that) he had a flat tire. |
| They said, "We're waiting for the bus." | They said<br>They told me | (that) they were waiting for the bus. |

**GRAMMAR NOTES**

- Use *said* to report a person's words.
- Use *told* to report a person's words and to report on who the person is speaking to.
- Use a noun (*Lee*, etc.) or an object pronoun (*her*, *me*, etc.) after *told*.

1. Bob _said_ he was changing his tire.
2. Yan _____ Lisa that she didn't belong to an auto club.
3. The teacher _____ us that there was a car in the parking lot with its lights on.
4. My friends _____ they wanted to buy a new car.

**B** Look at the quoted speech. Complete the reported speech. Use object pronouns. Then practice the conversations with a partner.

1. Mr. Ruiz stopped Liz in the hall. He said, "I need the key to the closet."

   Mr. Ruiz told _____ *her that he needed the key to the closet* _____ .

2. Tia phoned John. She said, "I'm calling about the homework."

   Tia told _____ .

3. Ken emailed his parents. He said, "I'm taking driving lessons."

   Ken told _____ .

4. Tasha texted my sister and me. She said, "I'm locked out of my apartment."

   Tasha told _____ .

**C** Work in a team. Edit the sentences. Write the corrected sentence.

1. He said that he is on Elk Road.  _He said that he was on Elk Road._
2. He says he was calling from a gas station.  _____
3. He said me that he had a flat tire.  _____
4. He said he is going to be late.  _____
5. He doesn't want us to wait, he said.  _____
6. We told we could wait.  _____

## 3 Listen for reported speech

🔊
1-25

**A** Listen to the conversations. Write the missing words.

1. David said that _____ he was _____ lost.

2. Patricia said that _____ a flat tire.

3. Lilia said that _____ for a tow truck.

4. Sam and Joe said that _____ in traffic.

5. They said that _____ the bus.

6. Larry _____ Cindy to call her sister. Cindy _____ her phone wasn't working.

7. Raul said that _____ to class. He also said that _____ out of gas.

8. Maria said that _____ an emergency kit.

**B** Work with a partner. Practice using quoted speech to talk about the people in 3A.

> What did David say?

> He said, "I'm lost."

## 4 Use reported speech to talk about others' ideas

**A** Write questions in the present tense or present continuous tense.

Do you prefer to travel alone or with friends?
Do you have a...?
Are you planning to...?
What is your favorite...?

**B** Work with a partner. Write two more questions.

**C** Work in a group of three. Ask and answer the questions in 4A and 4B. Then tell another group what your classmates said.

**Laura:** *Do you prefer to travel alone or with friends?*

## ▶▶ TEST YOURSELF

Close your book. Refer to your notes and write five sentences using the information you learned about your classmates. Use reported speech with *say* and *tell*.

Abby told me that she was planning to study for the nursing school entrance exam.

# 1 Learn ways to make travel plans

**A** Listen to the conversation. What website does Artie recommend?

1-26

**B** Listen again for the answers. Compare answers with your partner.

1-26

1. What kind of advice is Matthew asking for?
2. Where is Matthew planning to stay on his vacation?
3. Why is Matthew asking Artie for advice about his trip?

**C** Listen. Write the words Artie uses to make suggestions.

1-27

1. I'd check out the Seeta Airlines website _____ .
2. _____ finding a hotel there too.
3. Well, _____ definitely see the famous monuments!

# 2 Practice your pronunciation

**A** Listen to the pronunciation of the letter s in these sentences.

1-28

| Pronounced *s* | Pronounced *z* |
|---|---|
| Try thi<u>s</u> web<u>s</u>ite. | It i<u>s</u> ea<u>s</u>y to u<u>s</u>e. |

**B** Work with a partner. How do you think the letter *s* is pronounced in these words? Circle *s* or *z*.

1. use        s    z
2. hotels     s    z
3. sister     s    z
4. please     s    z
5. cats       s    z
6. does       s    z

**C** Listen and check. Then read the words in 2B with a partner.

1-29

# 3 Use reported speech with instructions

**A** Study the chart. Do you use *said* or *told* with *me* for reported instructions?

| Quoted speech | Reported speech |
|---|---|
| Laila said, "Use a mapping website." | Laila told me to use a mapping website. |
| Mati said, "Don't take Highway 75." | Mati told me not to take Highway 75. |
| Tomas said, "Please check the tires." | Tomas said to check the tires. |
| **GRAMMAR NOTES** | |
| Use an infinitive (*to* + verb or *not to* + verb) to report an instruction. | |

**B** Work with a partner. Rewrite Pedro and Lois' words in reported speech.

1. Pedro: "Please call me every day."  <u>Pedro told Lois to call him every day.</u>

2. Lois: "Don't worry!"  _____

3. Pedro: "Don't drive at night."  _____

4. Lois: "Please relax!"  _____

**C** Work with your classmates. Ask and answer the questions.

1. What do your friends often tell you to do?

2. What does your teacher always say to do?

3. What have you recently told yourself to start doing?

# 4 Building conversation skills

**A** Look at the picture and the conversation in 4B. What is the purpose of the conversation? How do you know?

1-30

**B** Listen to the sample conversation. How does the woman feel about her co-worker's suggestions? How do you know?

**A:** I'm planning a trip to Seattle. I've never been there!

**B:** I have. It's beautiful. If I were you, I'd look for a hotel away from downtown. It'll be cheaper.

**A:** That's a great suggestion; thanks. I'll probably look online.

**B:** Definitely. I'd try a couple of different sites, and different days, because the prices change. Why don't you talk to Elizabeth, too? She's been there.

**A:** That's funny—she told me to talk to you!

**IN OTHER WORDS...**

Making suggestions
*If I were you, I'd…*
*Why don't you…?*
*You might try…*
*You could…*
*How about trying…?*

**C** Role-play the situation below.

| Talk about | Roles | Instructions | Remember |
|---|---|---|---|
| Planning a trip | Co-worker | You want to leave the city for the weekend. You want to visit somewhere new. | Use key phrases from 4B |
| | Co-worker | Talk about the place your co-worker wants to go. Make suggestions. | Express interest |

AT WORK

## 5 Focus on listening for details

**A** Have you ever called a company or agency and had to use an automated message menu to get the information you needed? What happened? Discuss your experience with a partner.

*I had to call the jobs center/my credit card company/my children's health insurance company because....*

**B** Prepare to listen. Look at the choices in 5C. Predict the kind of company you will hear about on the message.

**C** Listen. Check (✓) the things you can do on this message system. Write an *X* for things you can't do. Compare your answers with a partner.

1-31

- ☐ Reserve a room.
- ☐ Get room service.
- ☐ Order a wedding cake.
- ☐ Get information about jobs.
- ☐ Find a nearby hotel.
- ☐ Hear the message again.

**D** Listen again. Write the numbers or the symbols the people should press.

1-31

1. Omar wants to have a company meeting at a Motel 212.    3
2. Elena wants to find a Motel 212 near her home.    _____
3. Billy wants a reservation at the Motel 212 in Dallas, Texas.    _____
4. Juanita needs to hear the choices again.    _____
5. Kevin is looking for a job at a Motel 212.    _____

## 6 Discuss

**A** Work with a group. Read the question and collaborate to make a chart. *Who can you tell to do something? Who should you ask to do something?*

- your little sister
- your supervisor
- a co-worker

**B** Report the results of your discussion to the class.

*Most people said that they ...*

---

## ▶▶ TEST YOURSELF

Assess your participation in the group and class discussions. Today I was able to...

- ☐ listen effectively
- ☐ make suggestions
- ☐ speak accurately
- ☐ ask questions

# 1 Read

**A** **Talk about the questions with your classmates.**

1. How has technology changed the ways people use transportation?
2. What are some new travel technologies you have used or heard of?

**B** **Read the definitions.**

mobility: (n) the ability to move around, or travel, easily

reduction: (n) the act of becoming smaller, less, or fewer

wireless: (adj) without wires

**C** **Preview the reading. Scan for numbers. Then mark the sentences *T* (true) or *F* (false).**

\_\_\_\_ 1. Members of New York City's bikesharing program rode more than 70,000 miles in the first season.

\_\_\_\_ 2. People in Washington D.C.'s bikesharing program drove cars more than 4 million fewer miles.

> **READER'S NOTE**
>
> Annotating a text can help the reader remember information and find details later. Annotation can include underlining, circling, or highlighting words or phrases, and writing questions or notes in the margin of a text.

**D** **Read the article. How are all of the new transportation systems alike?**

## Transportation and the Sharing Economy in the 21st Century

Nowadays, Americans are using new transportation services and options more, and driving less. This trend is due to rapid growth in smartphone
5 ownership, Internet access, and social media. In today's world:

Carsharing allows members to use cars without having to own them. Cars can be borrowed from and returned to a
10 central location. Bikesharing is now standard, and very popular, in many cities. In its first season alone, New York City's bikesharing program added more than 70,000 members. Ridesharing lets
15 ordinary drivers offer seats in their cars to others.

Real-time information allows riders to track the progress of buses and trains using their smartphones, thus saving
20 time and adding convenience.

The benefits of these new services include greater use of public transportation, and a reduction in number of vehicles owned. A 2013
25 survey of members of Washington, D.C.'s Capital Bikeshare program found a reduction in vehicle travel by members of an estimated 4.4 million miles.

30 Advocates for consumers and the environment encourage governments to: expand the availability of real-time transportation information, modernize laws on sharing rides and vehicles,
35 and make technology available to everyone. In addition, governments should think carefully about the community's needs before beginning major highway projects.

Source: *US PIRG*

**E** Read the article again. Does the writer offer suggestions? Underline the words that support your answer.

**F** Choose the words that describe the relationship between the concepts. Write the line number(s) where you found the answer. Talk about your answers with a partner.

1. Real-time information _____ smartphones. (line _____ )
   was developed before/is possible because of

2. Owners can offer seats in their vehicles _____ space. (line _____ )
   when they don't have/when they have

3. Sharing services are possible _____ technology. (line _____ )
   Instead of/because of

4. Bikeshare members in Washington D.C. used their vehicles less _____ they started using the bikesharing service. (line _____ )
   before/after

5. Governments should think about construction projects _____ they may not be necessary. (line _____ )
   because/unless

# 2 Word study

**A** Study the chart. Complete the sentences below.

| The suffix -*less* | | | |
| --- | --- | --- | --- |

The suffix -*less* means *without* or *not*. Add -*less* to the end of some nouns to form adjectives.

| Word | Meaning | Word | Meaning |
| --- | --- | --- | --- |
| wireless | without a wire | harmless | not harmful or dangerous |
| useless | without a use; not useful | speechless | unable to speak |

1. A cell phone is <u>useless</u> if you forget to charge the battery.

2. _____ communication has really changed the way people travel.

3. When he called, I couldn't think of anything to say. I was _____ with surprise.

4. My co-worker thinks ridesharing is dangerous, but I think it's _____ .

**B** Write a sentence about each topic. Use the underlined word in your sentence.

1. <u>driverless</u> cars

   _____

2. something <u>harmless</u> that some people think is dangerous

   _____

3. something people do even though it is <u>useless</u>

   _____

## 3 Talk it over

**A** Look at the graph and read the note. Complete the sentences. Use the words and numbers in the box. Answer the question.

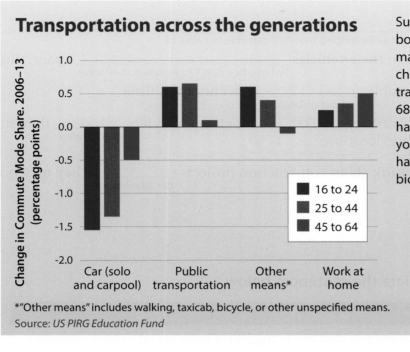

Surveys show that 'millennials' (those born between 1983 and 2000) have made the most changes in their choice of commuting mode, or way to travel to and from work. In 2012, only 68 percent of 19-year-olds in the U.S. had driver's licenses. Areas with many young people, like college towns, have had the biggest increase in bicycle commuting.

**READER'S NOTE**

Labels help the reader interpret the information in a chart. Labels include the horizontal (↔) and vertical (↕) chart labels, and 'keys' to explain colors used in the chart.

| increased | increase | decreased | 20th | 45 | 64 |

1. Commuting by car _decreased_ for every age group from 2006–2013.

2. Millennials are people born at the end of the _____ century.

3. Commuting by walking, bicycle, or other means increased for every group except people ages _____ to _____ .

4. Commuting by public transportation _____ for all groups.

5. There was an _____ in working at home for all groups.

6. How old are the youngest millennials this year?

**B** Work with a partner to discuss the questions.

1. What problems are caused by cars?

2. Why don't more people walk or bicycle to work?

3. What would convince you to try a new kind of travel or commuting?

4. What could your community do to encourage people to use public transportation?

 BRING IT TO LIFE

Think about your community. What changes in transportation have you noticed? Brainstorm a list of suggestions to make transportation better in your area.

**A** Listen to the informal staff meeting. What are they discussing?

1-32

**B** Listen to the informal meeting again. Then put a check next to each issue that is mentioned.

1-32

_____ number of chairs      _____ giving something to people who come

_____ getting a different room      _____ making copies tomorrow morning

_____ number of people not coming      _____ how to get cash to buy food

**C** Listen again. What was the suggestion for each issue? What were the consequences of each solution? Tell a partner what you heard.

1-32

**D** Read the chart. Discuss the questions below with your class.

| When you want to offer a suggestion, you can | |
|---|---|
| **Do this** | **Say this** |
| • Make eye contact.<br>• Lean toward the person.<br>• Raise your hand about six inches above the desk, with the index finger up. | Can I make a suggestion?<br>Why don't you/we…?<br>What do you think about…?<br>What if you/we…?<br>You know, we could…. |

1. Why is it important to make eye contact when you make a suggestion?

2. What else can you do with your hands when you make a suggestion?

3. In a formal situation, what should you not do when you make a suggestion?

**E** Work with a partner. Read the issues and make suggestions.

| Issues | Suggestions |
|---|---|
| No room is reserved | call… |
| Only three people have said they would come | ask… |
| Two people's supervisor told them not to | tell… |

**F** Have an informal planning meeting.

1. Work with a group. Decide on an event that is coming up at work.

2. Raise issues and suggest solutions. Use the ideas from your list and from this page. Discuss the consequences of each solution.

A: _We need to get ready for….What do we need to do?_

B: _One thing we need to do is…_

C: _What do you think about…?_

# TEAMWORK & LANGUAGE REVIEW

**A** Read the report of Maya's emergency call. Write the transcript: change the indirect speech to direct speech. Take turns role playing the conversation.

> Maya called 911 to report that she'd been in a car accident. She told the 911 operator that her name was Maya.
>
> The operator told her to try to stay calm. Maya said that there were two injured people, herself and her passenger, Ana. She said that Ana thought her leg was broken. The operator told Maya that she was calling the police and an ambulance. At that moment, Ana cried out that her leg was hurting very badly.
>
> Maya told Ana not to move. Just then, the ambulance arrived.

911: 911. What's your emergency?

Maya: I've been in a car accident.

911: What's _____

Maya: _____

**B** Look at the picture. Collaborate to describe what people said at the accident site. Write sentences with reported speech.

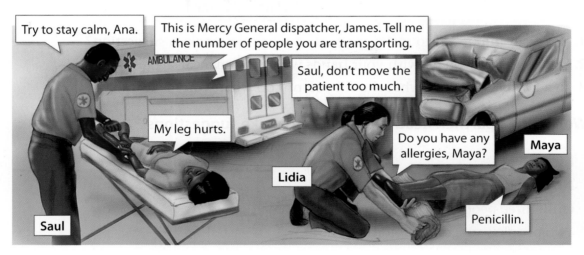

Try to stay calm, Ana.

This is Mercy General dispatcher, James. Tell me the number of people you are transporting.

AMBULANCE

Saul, don't move the patient too much.

My leg hurts.

Do you have any allergies, Maya?

Maya

Lidia

Penicillin.

Saul

*Saul told Ana to stay calm.*

**C** Work with your team. Write sentences with the correct pronouns.

1. The hospital dispatcher asked Saul and Lidia for information. What did he ask?
   He asked them to tell him the number of people they were transporting.

2. Saul told Ana something. What did he say?

3. Lidia asked Maya something. What did she ask?

4 Lidia cautioned Saul about something. What did she say?

**D** **Work in a team. Follow the steps below to complete the task.**

1. Assign team roles: manager, director, and actors.

2. Choose a type of vacation spot from the list on the right.

3. Write a conversation between the travel agent and the customer. The director gives directions for the task.

4. Rehearse your conversation. Act it out for the class.

> **Vacation places**
> • a quiet place
> • a place in the mountains
> • a place with a lot to do
> • a place at the beach

**E** **Interview three classmates. Write their answers.**

1. When you travel, do you like to go somewhere new or somewhere you've visited before? Why?

2. What is the best travel advice you have ever heard? Why?

3. Suppose you are going on a trip for a week. What are three things every traveler should take?

**F** **Report your results for Exercise E, #3 to the class. Make a bar graph with your class results.**

## PROBLEM SOLVING

1-33

**A** **Listen and read about Kofi.**

> Kofi needs to make a trip to another city for a job interview. The airfare would be about $400 roundtrip. He wants to drive because he thinks it will be cheaper. Kofi is worried about his car, though. It broke down last week, and he had to pay a mechanic $200 to fix it. It's running all right now, but the car is more than 10 years old. He wants to be sure he won't have another breakdown on his trip. His car also needs new tires. New tires would cost about $500. Kofi has $800 in the bank.

**B** **Work with your classmates. Respond to the prompts.**

1. Identify Kofi's problem.

2. Make a list of possible solutions for Kofi. For each one, discuss the consequences.

UNIT
# 4 Get the Job

**A LOOK AT**
- Career planning
- Past perfect
- Showing willingness

## LESSON 1 VOCABULARY

## 1 Identify career planning vocabulary

**A** Collaborate with your classmates. Brainstorm ways to get a job.

**B** Read the guide. Which of the steps have you done? What do you think is the best advice?

### Welcome to the Career Center!

**ORIENTATION GUIDE**

> At a career center, your first step should be to **see a career counselor**.

> If you are hoping to find a job quickly, you can **look at job listings** on a bulletin board or online.

> If you are thinking about your long-term plans and want to know what's possible, it's a good idea to **use the resource center**.

> In the center, you can go online to **take an interest inventory** to help you find out what kind of jobs and careers might be good for you.

> If you need to build up your skills to start on the career you want, ask about how you can **enroll in a training course** at your local college.

> If you need help paying for a course, you may be able to **apply for financial aid** to see if you can get a scholarship or a loan.

**C** Use context clues from 1B to match the words with the definitions.

_____ 1. career counselor

_____ 2. job listings

_____ 3. resource center

_____ 4. interest inventory

_____ 5. training course

_____ 6. financial aid

a. a person who helps you think about what job you want to do

b. different kinds of information in one location

c. help paying for school

d. questions to help you learn what job would be interesting for you

e. a class to learn skills for a specific job

f. all the jobs available

 **D** Listen for information about career services and job training. Check your work in 1C.
1-34

## 2 Learn more about career planning

**A** Look at the website. Complete the sentences. Use the words in 2A.

> **Continuing Education Dept ▼**
>
> **Career and Technical Training:** We offer more than 70 courses and programs to help you prepare for or advance in a career. <u>Click here for course listings and more information</u>.
>
> **Job Skills Workshops:** We offer monthly workshops for job seekers. We focus on the soft skills and employability skills that will help you get that job. Call us at 555-JOBS for information on the next workshop.
>
> **Internships:** Many of our partner employers offer internships for our students. Internships give you valuable work experience. For information, call our internship coordinator at 555-1188.
>
> **Online Courses:** If our in-person classes don't fit your schedule, consider taking an online training course. We offer hundreds of courses to help you get started on your career ladder. <u>Click here</u> to see our online course listings.
>
>
>
> **On-the-Job Training:** This one-day workshop will tell you all you need to know about getting training at your workplace. Make sure your basic skills are up-to-date and learn more about how to access "OJT". Walk-in workshops are held the first Thursday of every month at 7 p.m. at the college career center. No registration needed!
>
> **Apprenticeships:** Apprenticeships combine work experience with classroom training for jobs in many fields. They are a great way to get started. For information, <u>click here</u> to email our Apprenticeship Coordinator.

1. Loc just got a new job. He should ask his boss about ___on-the-job training___ .

2. Brenda is in an office assistant training program. She wants to get some experience. She should ask about an _____ .

3. Joe needs to work while he is learning. He should ask about an _____ .

4. Tonio is just starting to look for work. He should go to a _____ .

5. Mira stays at home with her children. She could try an _____ .

**B** Work with a partner. Practice the conversation. Use the words in 2A.

A: *I'm interested in an online course. What should I do?*

B: *You should click on the link for online course listings.*

**C** Conduct research with a team. Look at websites and community newsletters, and/or survey your classmates in order to report on the questions below.

What job training or career planning services are there in your area? Have you tried any of them? If so, what happened? If not, why not? What services would you like to see?

**D** Report the results of your research.

*Our team discovered that there is _____ in our area, but there isn't _____ . We have tried...*

---

## ▶▶ TEST YOURSELF

Work with a partner. Take turns reading and responding to the prompts in 1C.

**Partner A:** Read prompts 1–3. Partner B: Listen and write the vocabulary words.
**Partner B:** Read prompts 4–6. Partner A: Listen and write the vocabulary words.

# 1 Prepare to write

**A** Look at the email. Read the *To* and *Subject* lines. Talk about the questions with your class.

1. Why is Luis writing to Ms. Porter?    2. What do you think Ms. Porter's job is?

1-35

**B** Listen and read the email.

| | |
|---|---|
| Subject: | Re: Customer Service Representative position |
| From: | Luis Sanchez |
| Sent: | Wed 7/18/2018 |
| To: | lee.porter@vanitsdeptstore.biz |

Dear Ms. Porter:

I am writing in response to your job listing for a customer service representative. I have attached my resume.

I believe that my skills are a good match for the requirements of the position. I have two years' experience as a cashier, and I've completed a training class in customer skills. My computer skills are excellent, and I am fluent in English and Spanish. I am reliable, organized, and hardworking. I would be happy to provide a letter of recommendation.

I would like very much to meet with you to learn more about the position. I have listed my contact information on my resume. Thank you for considering me for this position.

Sincerely,

Luis Sanchez

**WRITER'S NOTE**

In a cover letter email, include information that is not in your resume.

**C** Mark the sentences *T* (true), *F* (false), or *NI* (no information).

__T__ 1. Luis is applying for a job at Vanit's.

_____ 2. Luis is writing to Ms. Porter because he met her at a job skills workshop.

_____ 3. Luis doesn't know how to use a cash register.

_____ 4. In his cover letter, Luis says why he is a good person for the job.

_____ 5. Luis has applied for several jobs.

**D** Study the email. Answer the questions.

1. Paragraph 1: What is Luis sending to Ms. Porter with this message?

2. Paragraph 2: What are Luis' skills and experience?

3. Paragraph 3: What does Luis want Ms. Porter to do?

## 2 Plan and write

### A Talk about the questions with your class. Take notes.

1. Would you like to apply for one of these jobs?

2. What job would you like to apply for at a company in your area?

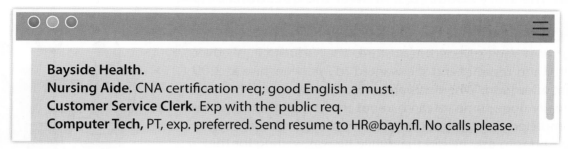

**Bayside Health.**
**Nursing Aide.** CNA certification req; good English a must.
**Customer Service Clerk.** Exp with the public req.
**Computer Tech,** PT, exp. preferred. Send resume to HR@bayh.fl. No calls please.

### B Write a cover letter email to Bayside Health or another company. Use the model email in 1B and your answers to the questions in 2A.

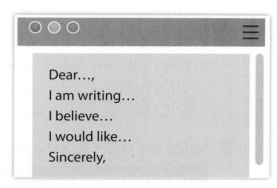

Dear...,
I am writing...
I believe...
I would like...
Sincerely,

## 3 Get feedback and revise

### A Use the editing checklist to review your writing. Check (✓) the true sentences.

☐ I stated my reason for writing.

☐ My message explains why I am applying for the job.

☐ I described my experience, skills, and personal characteristics.

☐ I signed my message.

### B Exchange emails with a partner. Read and comment on your partner's work.

1. Point out sentences that you think explain his or her qualifications for this position well.

*Your sentence, "I have experience..." describes your skills well.*

2. Point out a sentence where your partner could say more about himself/herself.

*I think you need to talk about _____ here.*

### C Use the checklist and your partner's feedback to revise your writing.

---

## ▸▸ TEST YOURSELF

Complete the following sentences. Share your responses with your teacher.

1. After this writing lesson, I can...
2. I need more help with...

## 1 Learn the past perfect

**A** Read the story about Luis. Answer the questions below.

On Thursday, Luis Sanchez got a phone call from Ms. Porter at Vanit's Department store. She had read Luis' cover letter and resume, and she wanted to interview him at 3:00 that afternoon. When Luis arrived for the interview, he had already done some research about the company, and he had completed the application online. He hadn't planned any questions to ask; he did that while he was waiting for the interview. Later, he wrote Ms. Porter a thank-you email.

1. What did Luis do before his interview?

2. What did he do while he was waiting to see Ms. Porter?

3. What did he do after the interview?

4. What two things did Ms. Porter do before she met Luis?

**B** Study the chart and the timeline. Underline the past perfect verbs in the story in 1A.

| The Past Perfect | | |
|---|---|---|
| **Affirmative and negative statements** | | |
| Luis | had completed | the application before he arrived. |
| He | hadn't planned | any questions before he arrived. |

**The Past Perfect**

Past ——————————×——————————————————×———————— Now

Ms. Porter read Luis' resume.      Ms. Porter called Luis.

**GRAMMAR NOTE**

Use the past perfect to show that an event happened before another event in the past. The past perfect shows the earlier event: *Ms. Porter had read Luis' resume before she called him.* (First Ms. Porter read Luis' resume. Then she called him.)

**C** Look at your answers to the questions in 1A. Complete the statements below.

**Language connection:** Two ways to use the past perfect

We can use the past perfect tense to talk about the order that events happened. When

sentences with the past perfect describe two events, we use the _____

(present perfect/past perfect)

tense for the event that happened first, and the _____ tense for the

(simple past/past perfect)

event that happened second. We use the past perfect for the _____ event and the

(earlier/later)

simple past for the _____ event.

(earlier/later)

**D** Complete the sentences with the past perfect form of the verbs in parentheses.

1. Ms. Porter called Luis after _she had read_ his resume. (read)
2. On Tuesday, Luis was worried because Ms. Porter _____ him. (not call)
3. Luis _____ at Vanit's website before Ms. Porter called him. (not look)
4. Luis _____ the company online before he went to the interview. (research)
5. The career counselor _____ Luis some advice before the interview. (give)

**E** Work with your class. What happened first? Circle *a* or *b*.

1. When I started the training class, I had already tried an online course.

    a. I started a training class.     b. I tried an online course.

2. Unfortunately, we arrived after the counselor had left.

    a. The counselor left.        b. We arrived.

3. After I sat down, I realized that I had forgotten to sign in.

    a. I sat down.           b. I forgot to sign in.

## 2 Learn past perfect questions

**A** Study the charts. Identify the verb that is used in short answers.

| Past Perfect Questions | |
| --- | --- |
| **Yes/No questions** | **Information questions** |
| A: Had you sent a resume before you called?<br>B: Yes, I had. or No, I hadn't. | A: How many jobs had you applied for before you got this job?<br>B: I had applied for four jobs before I got this job. |
| A: Had all the applicants emailed their resumes?<br>B: Yes, they had. or No, they hadn't. | A: Which classes had they taken before they started their internships?<br>B: They had taken computer classes before they started their internships. |

**B** Look at the answers. Then complete the questions with the past perfect.

**GRAMMAR NOTE**

No, I hadn't. NOT No, I'd not.

1. **A:** What _had you looked at_ before you applied for the job?

   **B:** Before I applied for the job, I had looked at the company's website.

2. **A:** _____ the training class before he applied for the job?

   **B:** Yes, he had. Pietro finished the training class two weeks ago.

3. **A:** How many people _____ before they interviewed you?

   **B:** I don't know how many people they had seen before they interviewed me.

4. **A:** Why _____ to Vanit's before she applied for the job there?

   **B:** She had gone to Vanit's to shop before she applied for the job there.

5. **A:** _____ in an office before you applied for the internship?

   **B:** No, I hadn't. I had worked in a restaurant, but not in an office.

## 3 Listen for the past perfect to determine the meaning

🔊 **A** **Listen to Mopati talk about his life. Circle the correct words.**

1-36

1. Before Mopati came to the U.S., he had always lived in a ( small town / big city ).

2. Now he lives in a ( small town / big city ).

3. Mopati had studied ( French / English ) before he came to the U.S.

4. He is studying ( French / Spanish ) now.

5. Before Mopati came to the U.S., he had always wanted to be a ( teacher / businessman ).

6. Now he wants to be a ( teacher / businessman ).

**B** **Work with a partner. Practice creating, asking, and answering questions about the information in 3A.**

*Before Mopati came to the U.S., where had he always lived?*

*He had always lived in a big city.*

## 4 Use the past perfect to talk about your life experience

**A** **Use the past perfect to complete the questions.**

1. What are two things you <u>had never done</u> (never do) before you came to the U.S.?

2. What is something you _____ (never see) before you came here?

3. What is one word you _____ (never hear) before you started this class?

**B** **Work with a partner. Write two more questions.**

1. Had you ever _____ before you came here?

2. Before you _____ , had you ever _____ ?

**C** **Work in a team. Ask and answer the questions in 4A and 4B. Take notes on your teammates' answers.**

**Ian:** *Had you ever eaten a hot dog before you came here?*

**Kevin:** *No, I hadn't. I had never heard of hot dogs.*

**Malia:** *Yes, I had. But only once.*

## ▶▶TEST YOURSELF

Close your book. Refer to your notes and write sentences using the information you learned about your classmates. Use the past perfect.

*Yulia had never visited a career center before she came to the U.S.*

## 1 Learn ways to respond to interview questions

**A** Listen to the conversations. Whose interview is longer, Ms. Jones' or Ms. Adams?

Ms. Jones

*Stopped 10/18*

www.casas.org

**B** Listen again for the answers. Compare answers with your partner.

1. What are the differences between the language Ms. Jones and Ms. Adams use?

2. In your opinion, which applicant does the interviewer think is better? How do you know?

**C** Listen. Write the words the applicants use to check understanding.

1. **A:** Tell me about your experience, Ms. Jones.

   **B:** _____ work experience?

2. **A:** How about training?

   **B:** _____ job training?

3. **A:** Tell me about your experience, Ms. Adams.

   **C:** _____ work experience?

4. **A:** How about training?

   **C:** _____ training related to restaurant work?

## 2 Practice your pronunciation

**A** Listen. Notice how speaker B uses rising intonation to check understanding.

1. **A:** Tell me about your experience.
   **B:** Do you mean in construction? ↗

2. **A:** What were your responsibilities?
   **B:** You mean at my last job? ↗

**B** Practice the conversations with a partner.

1. **A:** Tell me about your last job.
   **B:** My last job in an office?

2. **A:** What experience have you had?
   **B:** Experience in the U.S.?

3. **A:** Have you had any training?
   **B:** Computer training?

4. **A:** Do you have any questions?
   **B:** Questions about the job?

**C** Listen again. Repeat the sentences in 2B.

## 3 Compare the simple past, past perfect, and present perfect

**A** Study the chart. Mark the statements below *T* (true) or *F* (false).

| Simple past | Sam **got** his first job in a hospital in 2014. He **took** English classes from 2013 to 2016. |
|---|---|
| Past perfect | Sam **had** already **taken** a training class when he got the job, but he **hadn't worked** in a hospital before. |
| Present perfect | Sam **has worked** at the same hospital since 2014. He **has learned** a lot of English on the job. |

__F__ 1. Sam hasn't learned to speak English yet.

____ 2. Sam had already gotten his job before he started English classes.

____ 3. Sam got the job and then took a training class.

____ 4. Sam has worked at several hospitals.

____ 5. Sam is still a hospital worker.

**B** Check your understanding. Circle the correct verb. Ask and answer the questions.

1. Are you working now? If so, how long ( have / had ) you worked at your present job?

2. ( Had / Have ) you worked before you came to the U.S.? What did you do?

3. What was a job that you ( hadn't / didn't ) like?

## 4 Building conversation skills

**A** Look at the picture and the conversation in 4B. What is the purpose of the conversation? How do you know?

🔊 1-41 **B** Listen to the sample conversation. What qualifications does Luis have?

**A:** Tell me about your experience, Luis.

**B:** Do you mean with customers?

**A:** Yes, and other work experience, too.

**B:** Well, I've been a cashier for two years. Before that, I worked as a stock clerk.

**A:** How about training?

**B:** I completed a customer skills training class a year ago.

**A:** I see. Would you say you are a good team player?

**B:** Do you mean good at working with others? Yes, I do my best to contribute.

| IN OTHER WORDS... |
|---|

Checking understanding

| More formal | Less formal |
|---|---|
| *Do you mean…?* | *You mean…?* |
| *Is that…?* | *Like…?* |

**C** Role-play the situation below.

| Talk about | Roles | Instructions | Remember |
|---|---|---|---|
| Interview for a customer service position | Interviewer | Ask about the applicant's qualifications, including experience and training. | Use key phrases from 4B |
| | Applicant | Check your understanding of questions. Talk about your qualifications. | Check understanding |

# 5 Focus on listening for details

**A** Do you agree or disagree with the statement below? Why or why not? Discuss your opinion with a partner and state your reasons.

*It's a good idea to have a resume, even if you aren't looking for a job right now.*

**B** Prepare to listen. Look at the picture and read the sentences in 5C. Predict what you will hear.

**C** Listen. Circle the correct answers. Compare your answers with a partner.

1-42

1. Hanna ( has / hasn't ) finished her training class yet.
2. For the training class, Liz tells Hanna to write the month she started the class "to ( now / present )."
3. For her English classes, Hanna should write the name of the school, the place, the name of the ( teacher / class ), and the year she studied there.
4. Hanna finished high school in ( her country / the U.S. ).

# 6 Discuss

**A** Work with a group. Read the questions and collaborate to make a chart.

| What are some things you should do in a job interview? | What are some things you should not do in a job interview? |
| --- | --- |
|  |  |
|  |  |
|  |  |

**SPEAKING NOTE**

Encourage a team member or a group

*That's a great suggestion.*

*We're doing great!*

*What a good idea.*

*We're almost there/done/ finished.*

*Excellent idea!*

*Good work, team!*

A: *I think you should always bring a copy of your resume with you to an interview.*

B: *That's a great suggestion, Julia.*

C: *Good work, team! We're almost done!*

**B** Report the results of your discussion to the class.

*We think that one of the most important things to do in a job interview is …*

---

## ▶▶ TEST YOURSELF

Assess your participation in the group and class discussions. Today I was able to…

☐ listen effectively  ☐ check understanding

☐ speak accurately  ☐ ask questions

## **1** Read

### **A** Talk about the questions with your classmates.

1. What is the difference between a job and a career?

2. What skills do you think most employers are looking for?

### **B** Read the definitions.

field: (n) profession; area or subject of study or work

variety: (n) a number of different kinds of things

wages: (n) pay for a job

### **C** Preview the reading. Skim (quickly read) the first paragraph and the last paragraph. What do you think the article will be about? Circle the answer.

a. How to find training for a job you are interested in

b. How to find a job

c. How to go from a job to a career

**READER'S NOTE**

Numbered lists can show that the sequence or order of the items in the list is important, e.g., when steps should be taken in a specific order.

### **D** Read the article. What can you learn from government websites about careers?

**CAREER FINDERS**

| Home | Explore Careers ▼ | Training | Opportunities | Job Search | Resources |

Are you interested in finding a career? If so, here are the steps to take.

**1. Learn about yourself**

• Two good ways to learn about yourself are to take an interest inventory and a skills assessment. These assessments can help you learn about occupations that are a good match for you, and help you decide what additional training or experience you may need. You'll find a variety of assessments online through the U.S. Department of Labor.

• You can also do these assessments on your own. Make a list of your skills. Include your work skills (using a cash register, repairing cars), your life skills (using a computer, taking care of children, speaking different languages), and your "soft" skills (teamwork, reliable). Then make a list of jobs or careers that interest you.

**2. Research careers**

• The U.S. government's CareerOneStop website has profiles of more than 900 careers.

For each career, you'll find information on basic work activities, average wages, and employment projections, or how many openings there are expected to be in the future in each occupation.

• After you've identified a career[1], use the website to find out what education or training you need. Some careers, especially in medical or technical fields, require special training. A career counselor or a career website can help you find opportunities for training.

**3. Set your career goals**

• Think about where you would like to be in one year, and in five years. What are the steps you need to take to reach your goal? It may be learning a new skill, or obtaining a professional license or certificate. New experiences, including volunteering in your community or joining a professional group, can help too. Be patient. Moving from a job into a career takes time and effort. But it's worth it!

[1]identify a career: find or choose a career

SOURCE: *U.S. Department of Labor; Career One stop*

**E** Use the graphic organizer to take notes on the information in the article.

| To learn about yourself | To research careers | To set goals |
|---|---|---|
| 1. | 1. | 1. |
| 2. | 2. | 2. |
| 3. | 3. | 3. |

**F** Scan the article. Circle the correct words.

1. ( An occupation / A career ) describes a field of work, including the kinds of work and workplaces that go with it.

2. The article says that taking care of children can be a ( life skill / soft skill ).

3. Employment projections tell you which jobs will probably ( pay well / grow ) over the next ten years.

4. The *CareerOneStop* website has profiles of ( hundreds / thousands ) of careers.

# 2 Word study

**A** Study the chart. Complete the sentences below.

### suffixes -er and -ee

The suffix -er can be added to the end of some verbs to show the person who performs an action.

The suffix -ee can be added to the end of some verbs to show the person who receives the result of the action. An **employer** employs an **employee**.

| Verbs | Nouns | |
|---|---|---|
| employ | employer | employee |
| train | trainer | trainee |
| pay | payer | payee |

1. Ms. Adams has been an <u>employee</u> here for several years. Her _____ thinks that she is an excellent worker.

2. Mr. Johnson is a computer _____ at his company. He has 15 _____ in his class right now.

3. The person who receives a check is the _____ . The person who writes it is the _____ .

**B** Write a sentence about each topic. Use the underlined word in your sentence.

1. something an <u>interviewer</u> should not ask

_____

2. something an <u>interviewee</u> should not ask

_____

## 3 Talk it over

**A** Look at the graph and read the note. Complete the sentences and answer the questions.

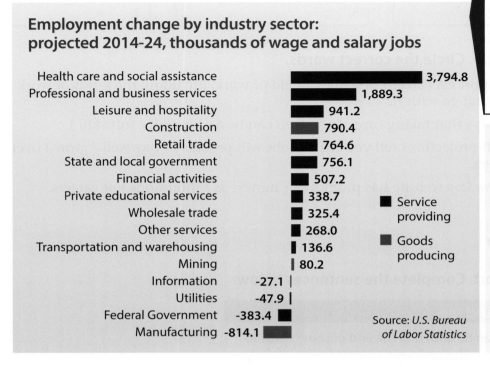

Employment change by industry sector: projected 2014-24, thousands of wage and salary jobs

|  |  |
|---|---|
| Health care and social assistance | 3,794.8 |
| Professional and business services | 1,889.3 |
| Leisure and hospitality | 941.2 |
| Construction | 790.4 |
| Retail trade | 764.6 |
| State and local government | 756.1 |
| Financial activities | 507.2 |
| Private educational services | 338.7 |
| Wholesale trade | 325.4 |
| Other services | 268.0 |
| Transportation and warehousing | 136.6 |
| Mining | 80.2 |
| Information | -27.1 |
| Utilities | -47.9 |
| Federal Government | -383.4 |
| Manufacturing | -814.1 |

■ Service providing
■ Goods producing

Source: *U.S. Bureau of Labor Statistics*

**Labor projections**
From 2014 to 2024, healthcare and social assistance jobs are expected to account for over one third of all job growth. Health care occupations are projected to add 2.3 million jobs, about 1 in 4 of all new jobs. Workers age 55 and above are expected to be almost one quarter of the labor force in 2024.

1. The job projections cover the period from 2014 to _2024_ .
2. Most new jobs are expected to be in _____ occupations, not in goods producing fields.
3. About ¼ of all new jobs are expected to be in _____ occupations.
4. The industry sector with the largest projected job loss is _____ .
5. What sector is mentioned in both the graph and the note? _____
6. What issue is mentioned in the note but not in the graph? _____

**B** Think about the questions. Discuss your ideas with your classmates.

1. What jobs do you think will probably grow in your area?
2. Why do you think those jobs will grow?
3. What advice would you give a person who is going to graduate from high school this year, about jobs and careers?
4. What advice would you give a friend who would like to move from a job to a career in your area?

**C** Talk about your answers with your classmates.

 BRING IT TO LIFE

Find a skills inventory or career-interest inventory at the library, at a career center, or on the Internet. Complete the inventory. What careers does it tell you to look at? Do you agree? Talk about your reasons with your classmates.

**A** Listen to the conversation. Who is talking?

1-43

**B** Listen to the conversation again. Mark the sentences *T* (true) or *F* (false).

1-43

  _F_   1. Larry is Ms. Lopez's supervisor.

  ____   2. The professional development office is the company's training office.

  ____   3. Ms. Lopez doesn't think Larry should apply for the training program.

  ____   4. Larry is interested in the suggestion Ms. Lopez is making.

**C** Listen again. How does Larry show his interest in what Ms. Lopez is saying? Tell a partner what you heard.

1-43

**D** Read the chart. Discuss the questions below with your class.

| When you want to show a willingness to learn, you can | |
| --- | --- |
| **Do this** | **Say this** |
| • Research job information or skills on the Internet<br>• Read company newsletters and bulletin boards<br>• Volunteer for a project at work<br>• Repond positively when you are offered an opportunity | I don't know how to _____ but I would like to learn.<br>I've been researching ___ and I've learned that …<br>Can you teach me how to…<br>Are there any classes I can attend?<br>I am always interested in the chance to learn something new.<br>I would be very interested in … |

1. Why is it important to show a willingness to learn at work?

2. What kinds of things can you learn from online tutorials?

3. What are other ways you can show that you are willing to learn at work?

**E** Work with a partner. Take turns offering an opportunity and responding to the offer.

> **Opportunity**
> Supervisory training
> On-the-job training
> Financial aid for a training class at the college

**F** Have a conversation.

1. Work with a group to make a list of opportunities employers can offer their employees.

2. Choose one person to be a supervisor. Everyone else take turns meeting with the supervisor to hear about one of the opportunities. Use the ideas from your list and from this page. Ask a question about the opportunity.

  A: *Thanks for coming. I'd like to talk to you about an opportunity to…*

  B: *Thank you. I'm…*

# TEAMWORK & LANGUAGE REVIEW

CPR course

home health
care aide

CNA training

CNA position

nursing degree

nursing job

**A** Look at Al's career path. Collaborate to create a timeline showing six or more steps on Al's career path.

```
                    Arrived in U.S.
◄─────────────────────┼──────────────────────────────────►
                     1990
```

**B** Write at least six past perfect questions about Al's career path. Use the question frames and verbs below. Compare questions with your teammates.

| work as | start | finish | take | study | graduate |
|---------|-------|--------|------|-------|----------|

How long had Al _____ before he _____ ?

Had he _____ before he _____ ?

**C** Take turns asking and answering your questions from B with your team.

A: *Had Al finished nursing school before he worked as a CNA?*

B: *No, he hadn't.*

C: *How long had he been a CNA before he started nursing school?*

D: *He had been a CNA for…*

**D** Collaborate to complete the paragraph about Irene's career path. Use the past perfect or present perfect of the verbs you see.

Irene _____ never _____ about a career before she got her present job in a bakery. (think)
        1            2

She _____ as a cashier in a retail store before she got her bakery job. (work)
    3

In her present job as a baker's assistant, she _____ a lot about baking. (learn)
                                    4

Before she got this job, she _____ always _____ that machines made bread. (believe)
                      5               6

Since she started this job, she _____ a lot about becoming a baker herself someday. (think)
                               7

**E** Work in a team. Follow the steps below to complete the task.

1. Assign team roles: manager, writer, editor, presenter.
2. Think of a career path that you know well. (Not Al's or Irene's!)
3. Collaborate on a story about a person on that career path.
4. Read your story to the class.

**F** Interview three classmates. Write their answers.

1. Before you came to the U.S., what kind of career training had you had? What about since you came to the U.S.?
2. Have you ever made a list of your skills?
3. In your opinion, what is the most important thing people should do at a job interview?

**G** Report your results for Exercise F, #1 to the class. Make a chart with your class results.

## PROBLEM SOLVING

**A** Listen and read about Jin.

1-44

> Jin works in her family's restaurant. She's worked there for three years, and she's very good at her job. She has learned to cook, wait on customers, use the cash register, and keep track of the restaurant's accounts. Jin likes helping her family, but she is thinking about her future. Before her family decided to come to the U.S., she had studied accounting at a technical school. Jin would like to work in the accounting field, but she doesn't know how to look for a job. She's never had to write a resume, and she has never visited a career center or had a job interview.

**B** Work with your classmates. Respond to the prompts.

1. Identify Jin's problem.
2. Make a list of possible actions Jin could take. Discuss the possible consequences of each possible action.

UNIT

**5** Safe and Sound

**A LOOK AT**
- Safety
- Modals for advice
- Asking for clarification

## LESSON **1** VOCABULARY

AT WORK

# **1** Identify safety hazards and warnings

**A** Collaborate with your classmates to answer the questions.

Which things in the picture could be dangerous? What problem does each danger cause?

Attention all Employees! Only **authorized** personnel may use the materials stored in this area. Do not enter this area if you are not authorized. These materials must be handled with extreme **caution**. If equipment is broken or damaged, do not use! Safety is everyone's business. Make it yours!

**B** Use context clues. Mark the words in the notice or in the picture that help you understand the bold words in the text. Compare your ideas with a partner.

**C** Complete the statements with the words from the picture. Then listen and check.

2-02

1. It's dangerous to breathe in *poisonous fumes* .

2. Never have a fire around _____ liquids.

3. Only authorized employees can open the _____ .

4. Never use a piece of equipment with a _____ .

5. A yellow sign with three black triangles means the container's contents are _____ .

6. _____ don't catch fire, but they can burn your skin.

7. Put up a warning sign when the floor is _____ .

8. An employee who uses a _____ could fall and be seriously hurt.

**D** Ask and answer the questions with a partner.

1. Where do you see safety or warning signs?

2. What safety or warning signs have you seen at or near your school?

## 2 Learn about safety precautions

**A** Look at the safety flyer. Match the safety advice with the examples.

### Four Ways to Be Safe on Campus

**Be Alert**
Keep your eyes open. Watch for anything unusual in the area around you.

**Avoid Isolated Areas**
Walk in areas where there are people around you, especially at night.

**Report Suspicious Activities Immediately**
If you see something, tell someone about it.

**Prevent Accidents**
Follow all safety rules, and report dangerous situations.

___c___ 1. Be alert.

_____ 2. Report suspicious activities.

_____ 3. Avoid isolated areas.

_____ 4. Prevent accidents.

a. You report broken equipment.

b. You walk on a busy street.

c. You notice a package with no owner.

d. Someone is following a student.

**B** Work with a partner. Practice the conversation. Use the words in 2A.

A: *I told someone about something I saw.*

B: *That's good. Everyone should report suspicious activities immediately.*

**C** Conduct research with a team. Survey your classmates in order to report on the questions below.

1. Which of the safety hazards, warning signs, or situations from this lesson have you seen at home, work, or school? Describe one situation or hazard.

2. How can people prevent accidents at home? At work? At school?

3. Which things in your home have warning or caution labels?

**D** Report the results of your research.

*Our team has seen...*

*People can prevent accidents if they ...*

*In our homes, ....have warning labels.*

## ▶▶ TEST YOURSELF

Work with a partner. Take turns reading and responding to the prompts in 1C.

**Partner A:** Read prompts 1–4. Partner B: Listen and write the vocabulary words.
**Partner B:** Read prompts 5–8. Partner A: Listen and write the vocabulary words.

## 1 Prepare to write

### A Talk about the questions with your class.

1. What types of weather emergencies occur in your area?
2. Have you ever made an emergency plan? Why or why not?

NEED HELP?

**Weather emergencies**
blizzard
hurricane
wildfire
tornado
flood

### 🔊 B Listen and read the emergency plan.
2-03

| | Hurricane Emergency Plan<br>by the Duval Family |
|---|---|
| I. Before | A. Make emergency kit Supplies: |
| |     1. we have: canned food, can opener, blankets, radio |
| |     2. to buy: batteries, first-aid kit, bottled water, |
| |         flashlights |
| | B. Get information |
| |     1. Learn evacuation routes |
| |     2. Identify emergency contact person |
| II. During | 1. Stay indoors and away from windows |
| | 2. Don't use candles or electrical equipment |
| | 3. Watch for tornadoes |
| | 4. Listen for warnings |
| III. After | A. Check radio or TV for instructions |
| | B. Check house for damage |

**WRITER'S NOTE**
Use phrases or short sentences when you make an outline. You don't have to use articles (*a, an, the*) or ending punctuation.

### C Study the emergency plan. Mark the statements *T* (true), *F* (false), or *NI* (no information).

___F___ 1. The Duval family already has a first-aid kit.

_____ 2. The family needs to buy batteries.

_____ 3. In the Duvals' area, tornadoes might occur during hurricanes.

_____ 4. The Duvals live in Florida.

## 2 Plan and write

**A Talk about the questions with your class. Take notes.**

1. What types of emergencies do people in your area prepare for?

2. What steps should people take to prepare for different kinds of emergencies?

3. Where can you get information about possible emergencies in your area?

**B Outline a plan for an emergency in your area. Use the model emergency plan in 1B and your answers to the questions in 2A and below.**

Part 1: What should you do before the emergency?
  What do you have? What should you buy?

Part 2: How can you stay safe during the emergency?

Part 3: What should you do after the emergency?

| | [Title] |
|---|---|
| I. Before | A. |
| | B. |
| II. During | A. |
| | B. |
| III. After | A. |
| | B. |

## 3 Get feedback and revise

**A Use the editing checklist to review your writing. Check (✓) the true sentences.**

☐ I gave my plan a title.

☐ I used phrases or short sentences.

☐ I followed the format for an outline.

☐ I included plans for before, during, and after an emergency.

**B Exchange plans with a partner. Read and comment on your partner's work.**

1. Point out examples of good organization.

   *Your plan to…before you…is a really good idea.*

   *The difference between…and…is very clear.*

2. Give feedback about the plan. Check your understanding.

   *I'm not sure I understand this part of the plan.*

**C Use the checklist and your partner's feedback to revise your writing.**

## ▶▶ TEST YOURSELF

Complete the following sentences. Share your responses with your teacher.

1. After this writing lesson, I can…
2. I need more help with…

## 1 Use *have to*, *not have to*, *have got to*, *must*, and *must not*

**A** Read the article. Answer the questions below.

### City Official Says Silton Bay Must Prepare for Major Earthquake

**Mayor Sam Andreas announced** today that Silton Bay is not prepared for a major earthquake. Andreas said, "People think that they don't have to worry about a major earthquake here, but they're wrong."

According to Andreas, everyone in the area has to be prepared. "Every resident, every family, every business has to have an emergency plan. We must buy emergency food and medical supplies. We've all got to plan where to go if our homes are damaged."

Andreas stressed that earthquakes cannot be predicted. "But we must not think that we are safe just because we haven't had an earthquake in many years," he said.

1. Who is the city official in the headline of this news story?
2. In the first paragraph, what does the mayor say that people have to do?
3. In the last paragraph, what may people believe about their safety?

**B** Study the charts. Underline the examples of *have to*, *have got to*, *must*, and *must not* in the article in 1A.

| Have to, have got to, and must for necessity and prohibition | | |
|---|---|---|
| **Necessity** | | |
| People | have to/have got to/must | prepare for emergencies. |
| **Lack of Necessity** | | |
| People in Florida | don't have to | prepare for earthquakes. |
| **Prohibition** | | |
| After an earthquake, people | must not | enter a damaged home. |

**C** Look at your answers to the questions in 1A. Complete the statements below.

### Language connection: Necessity and prohibition

We can use *have to* and *must* to talk about things that are necessary and things that are prohibited. *Have to* _____ the same meaning as *must*. *Don't have to*
(has/does not have)
_____ the same meaning as *must not*. _____ has the same meaning
(has/does not have)                    (have/have got to)
as *must*. To say that an action is not allowed, or prohibited, we use _____ .
(don't have to/must not)
To say an action is not _____ we use *don't have to*.
(necessary/prohibited)

**D** Complete the sentences with *have to, don't have to, have got to,* or *must not.*

1. You <u>must not</u> go out of the house during a hurricane.
2. I _____ buy any canned food. I have some already.
3. She _____ worry about floods. She lives in a safe area.
4. People _____ use electrical equipment during a hurricane. It's extremely dangerous.
5. A tornado is coming! We _____ go outside.
6. We _____ watch the news on TV. We can listen to it on the radio instead.

**E** Mark the statements *N* (necessary), *NN* (not necessary), or *P* (prohibited).

<u>P</u>  1. That chemical has poisonous fumes. You must not use it in the house.
_____  2. We've got to prepare for emergencies.
_____  3. You don't have to be afraid to walk at night when you walk with friends.
_____  4. We must fix the broken ladder before we use it.
_____  5. You must not stand near a window in a tornado.

## **2** Use *have to* and *must* in the past

**A** Study the chart. Circle the correct words in the sentences below.

| Necessity in the past | |
| --- | --- |
| **Now** | **In the past** |
| This year, Rosa has to buy new supplies. | Last year, she had to buy a first-aid kit. |
| They've got to buy fresh batteries. | They had to buy a ladder last month. |
| They must check the house for storm damage. | Her husband had to repair the roof last August. |
| Their son doesn't have to go to school today because of the storm. | He didn't have to go to school yesterday either. |

**GRAMMAR NOTE**

There are no past forms of *must* or *have got to* to express necessity. Use *had to* instead.

1. Rosa and her family ( had to / have to ) repair the roof last year.
2. She ( doesn't have to / didn't have to ) replace any windows last year.
3. They always ( had to / have to ) check for damage after every storm.
4. Their neighbor ( had to / must ) remove a tree from his roof after the storm.
5. Hurricane season is beginning, so they ( had to / must ) make an emergency plan.
6. Before it storms, her husband ( has got to / had to ) make sure their insurance is up-to-date.

**B** Work with a partner. Talk about childhood experiences.

A: *When you were a child, did you have to _____ ?*
B: *Yes, I did. What about you?*
A: *I didn't have to _____ , but I had to _____ .*

**NEED HELP?**

Childhood experiences
*go to school on _____*
*work at home _____*
*walk _____*
*_____ when you were sick*

# 3 Listen for the verb to determine the meaning

🔊
2-04

**Listen to the emergencies. Choose the sentences with the same meaning. Circle *a* or *b*.**

1. a. We have to call 911.
2. a. We have got to evacuate the area.
3. a. Children must go to the basement.
4. a. Residents have to leave the area.
5. a. Last year, people had to leave their homes.
6. a. Most people had to buy emergency supplies.

b. We don't have to call 911.
b. We don't have to evacuate the area.
b. Children must not go to the basement.
b. Residents don't have to leave the area.
b. Last year, people didn't have to leave their homes.
b. Most people didn't have to buy emergency supplies.

# 4 Use *have to* to talk about your life experience

**A Complete the questions. Use the words in the box.**

| in your country | in the U.S. | now |
|---|---|---|
| before you came here | | |

1. What did you have to do _____ ?
2. Do you have to do that _____ ?
3. What didn't you have to do _____ ?
4. Do you have to do that _____ ?

**B Work with a partner. Write two more questions.**

1. Did you have to _____ in your country?
2. Do you have to _____ now?

**C Work in a team. Ask and answer the questions in 4A and 4B. Take notes on your teammates' answers.**

Lisa:      *What did you have to do in your country?*

Leopold:   *I had to go to the market every day.*

Lisa:      *Do you have to do that now?*

## ▶▶ TEST YOURSELF

Close your book. Refer to your notes and write six sentences using the information you learned about your classmates. Use *have to* in the present and past.

*Eliane didn't have to take the bus to work in her country, but now she has to take the bus every day.*

# 1  Learn ways to report unsafe conditions

**A** Listen to the conversation. Who is Mr. Jenks?
2-05

**B** Listen again for the answers. Compare answers with your partner.
2-05

1. What is the first problem Suki reported?

2. What is the second problem she reported?

3. Does Mr. Jenks appreciate Suki's information? How do you know?

**C** Listen. Write the words Suki uses to report unsafe conditions.
2-06

1. _____ a problem in the basement.

2. Well, _____ another thing.

3. There's an oil spill in one corner. _____ one of the containers is leaking.

# 2  Practice your pronunciation

**A** Listen to the conversation. Listen to the pronunciation of *-ough* in each word.
2-07

A: Look—I bought enough water for four people for three days.

B: Do you think that's enough?

A: Yes. We should also have canned or dried food, though.

B: I'll buy that, and a first-aid kit. Then we'll be through with our emergency kit.

**B** Listen again. Match each word with *-ough* with a word that has a similar sound.
2-07

___b___ 1. bought            a. stuff

_____ 2. through          b. saw

_____ 3. enough           c. go

_____ 4. though           d. too

**C** Read the conversation with a partner. Then listen and check your pronunciation.
2-08

A: *I bought a new lock for the restricted area.*

B: *Do you think one lock is enough?*

A: *Yes, if we put it through the handles of both doors.*

B: *Good. We still need a lock for the supply cabinet, though.*

## 3 Use *should have*

**A** Study the chart. Where are the boxes?

| Should have | |
|---|---|
| **Affirmative statements** | **Negative statements** |
| You should have put the boxes in the storeroom. | You should not have left them in the hall. |
| He should have listened to his manager. | He shouldn't have forgotten the boxes. |

**GRAMMAR NOTE**

Use *should (not) have* + past participle to give an opinion about a situation in the past.

**B** Check your understanding. Write statements with *should have* or *shouldn't have*.

1. I didn't report the problem. <u>You should have reported the problem</u>

2. We went into the restricted area. _____

3. They didn't wear protective gloves. _____

4. She used a lamp with a frayed cord. _____

**C** Work with your classmates. Ask and answer the questions.

1. Have you ever made a mistake at school? What did you do? What should you have done?

2. Have you ever reported a problem at work, at school, or at home? What happened?

## 4 Building conversation skills

**A** Look at the picture and the conversation in 4B. What is the purpose of the conversation? How do you know?

🔊 **B** Listen to the sample conversation. What is suspicious? Why?

2-09

**A:** Hi. I want to report something suspicious.

**B:** OK; I appreciate it. What did you see?

**A:** I noticed a package near bus stop number 11. It's been there for a while and no one is near it.

**B:** OK, hmm. We'll send someone to take a look.

**A:** Also, there's a broken light. It's dark and isolated at night.

**B:** Someone should have fixed that. I'll let Maintenance know.

**IN OTHER WORDS...**

Reporting a problem
*I'd like to report…*
*I want to report…*
*There seem(s) to be…*
*I noticed…*

**C** Role-play the situation below.

| Talk about | Roles | Instructions | Remember |
|---|---|---|---|
| Problems at a park | Park visitor | Report safety hazards: broken glass near the playground; trash can is full, trash on the ground. | Use key phrases from 4B<br>Express interest |
| | Park employee | Thank the visitor. Agree to: send someone to clean up the glass, tell the groundskeepers about the trash. | |

# 5 Focus on listening for details

**A** Check (✓) the job you think is the safest. Talk about your answer with your class.

☐ teacher ☐ construction worker ☐ computer worker

**B** Prepare to listen. Look at the picture and read the sentences in 5D. Predict what you will hear in the interview.

🔊 2-10 **C** Listen to the news story. Check (✓) the occupation that is NOT mentioned.

☐ librarians ☐ teachers
☐ nurses ☐ news reporters
☐ computer occupations ☐ construction workers

🔊 2-10 **D** Listen again. Complete the sentences. Compare your answers with a partner.

1. People working in education had _____ injuries or illnesses for every 10,000 workers.

2. Police and protective service workers had almost _____ injuries and illnesses per 10,000 people.

3. On average, construction workers missed _____ work days a year.

4. Computer and math occupations had the _____ injury rate.

5. They missed on average _____ days per year.

# 6 Discuss

**A** What makes jobs safe or unsafe? Collaborate with a group to make a chart. Include ideas on other occupations.

- Nursing
- Protective services
- Construction

A: *I think nursing is often not safe because…*
B: *That's interesting. Why do you think so?*

**B** Report the results of your discussion to the class.

*We think that nursing is not always safe because …*

> **SPEAKING NOTE**
>
> **Understand other points of view**
> *That's interesting.*
> *Why do you think so?*
> *Can you say a little more about that?*
> *I see. I'm not sure I understand where you're coming from.*

---

## ▶▶ TEST YOURSELF

Assess your participation in the group and class discussions. Today I was able to…

☐ listen effectively ☐ build on my classmates' ideas
☐ speak accurately ☐ ask questions

# 1 Read

## A Talk about the questions with your classmates.

1. What do you think are the most common injuries at work? At home?

2. How can people try to prevent injuries at work and at home?

## B Read the definitions.

keep track of: (v) to watch, keep a record of

sprain: (n) an injury caused by suddenly twisting or turning a part of the body

strain: (n) an injury caused by using a part of the body too much

## C Preview the reading. Where does the data come from?

a. The U.S. Department of Labor and the U.S. Sports Safety Commission

b. The U.S. Department of Labor and the Consumer Product Safety Commission

c. The U.S. Consumer Product Safety Commission

## D Read the article. What is the writer's purpose? Does the writer achieve this purpose?

> **READER'S NOTE**
>
> Facts, data and quotations *support* the writer's point of view.
>
> Advice and opinions *express* the writer's point of view.

# My Point of View   By Dr. Rita Ochoa

1 Accidents and injuries can happen at any time —at home or at work. The more you know about common injuries and accidents, the better you can avoid and prevent them. Safety
5 is everyone's responsibility!

The U.S. Department of Labor keeps track of time people take off from work because of injuries and illnesses. In a recent survey, sprains and strains were the most common reasons
10 given for workers' needing to take time off. The majority of injuries were caused by falls, accidents with objects or equipment, or overexertion.

Injuries at home are often caused by everyday
15 items. According to the U.S. Consumer Product Safety Commission, stairs and ramps are two of the most hazardous parts of the home. Tools and household containers account for[1] many emergency room visits. One of the most
20 dangerous activities is playing basketball!

I believe that most accidents can be prevented. Everyone should be aware of and follow safety rules and procedures. Use the proper equipment (and use it properly),
25 whether it's seatbelts or a child safety seat in your car, or equipment at work. Read the directions on cleaning chemicals, medicines, and tools. Use handrails on stairs and caution on slippery floors. Basic precautions are the best
30 way to protect yourself from injury—use them!

[1]account for: to be responsible for

Source: *National Electronic Injury Surveillance System (NEISS)*

**E** Read the article again. Which paragraphs give you the author's point of view? Underline the words that support your answer.

**F** Mark the statement *T* (true), *F* (false), or *NI* (no information). For each true or false answer, write the line number(s) where you found the answer.

_____ 1. At work, overexertion causes more injuries than falls. (line _____ )

_____ 2. Stairs, ramps, landings and floors accounted for over 2.5 million injuries. (line _____ )

_____ 3. The writer believes that it is not possible to prevent most accidents. (line _____ )

_____ 4. The writer describes several ways to stay safe. (line _____ )

_____ 5. The writer believes that it is easier to prevent accidents at home than at work. (line _____ )

## 2 Word study

**A** Study the chart. Complete the sentences below.

### The suffix -ous

The suffix -ous means *full of* or *having the quality of*. There is sometimes a spelling change: *caution—cautious*

| Noun | Adjective | Verb | Adjective |
|------|-----------|------|-----------|
| caution | cautious | vary | various |
| danger | dangerous | continue | continuous |
| hazard | hazardous | | |
| disaster | disastrous | | |

1. Don't leave things on the stairs. It's a safety ( hazard / hazardous ).

2. Be ( caution / cautious ) around flammable liquids. They're a ( danger / dangerous ) at many workplaces.

3. That frayed electrical cord is ( danger / dangerous ).

4. ( Hazard / Hazardous ) chemicals are stored in a locked cage.

5. During a safety check, we discovered ( vary / various ) safety violations.

**B** Write a sentence about each topic. Use the underlined word in your sentence.

1. an example of a <u>disastrous</u> weather event

_____

2. something you are always <u>cautious</u> with, or doing

_____

3. something you have seen <u>continuous</u> improvement in

_____

## 3 Talk it over

**A** Look at the graph and read the note. Complete the sentences and answer the questions.

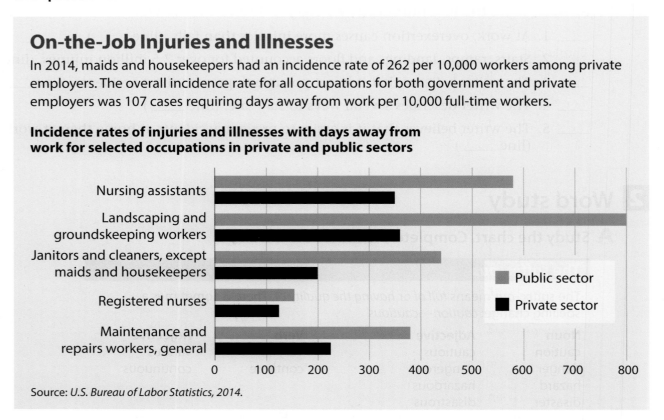

### On-the-Job Injuries and Illnesses

In 2014, maids and housekeepers had an incidence rate of 262 per 10,000 workers among private employers. The overall incidence rate for all occupations for both government and private employers was 107 cases requiring days away from work per 10,000 full-time workers.

**Incidence rates of injuries and illnesses with days away from work for selected occupations in private and public sectors**

Source: *U.S. Bureau of Labor Statistics, 2014.*

1. For all full-time workers, the average number of job-related injuries and illnesses requiring days away from work per 10,000 workers was _____ .

2. The rate for landscapers was about _____ times as high in private sector jobs as in governments jobs.

3. Which had the higher rate of incidents among private employers: janitors and cleaners, or maids and housekeepers? _____

4. Which occupation had the highest incidence rate in government jobs? _____

5. Did jobs in government or private sector have more injuries and illnesses? _____

**B** Work with a partner to discuss the questions.

1. Why does the government report workplace safety data to the public?

2. What are some things employers should do to keep workers safe?

3. What laws do you know that are designed to keep people safe?

4. Why should businesses care about the safety of their workers?

---

 BRING IT TO LIFE

Search online. What are the most important safety precautions for the workplace, school, and home? Discuss with your clasmates.

**A** Listen to the staff meeting. What are they discussing? (2-11)

**B** Listen to the staff meeting again. Complete the workers' safety laws. (2-11)

Employers…

1. must provide a _____ .
2. must provide safety _____ .
3. must protect workers from poisonous _____ .

Workers…

4. must be trained in a _____ .
5. can request a _____ inspection.
6. _____ worry about retaliation.

See something unsafe? Ask!

**C** Listen again. Check your answers in B. Compare your answers with a partner. (2-11)

**D** Read the chart. Discuss the questions below with your class.

| When you don't hear or understand the speaker you can | |
| --- | --- |
| **Do this** | **Say this** |
| • Make eye contact and raise your shoulders.<br>• Cup your hand behind your ear.<br>• Raise your hand.<br>• Raise your index finger. | Excuse me?<br>What was that?<br>I'm sorry I missed that…<br>Could you repeat that slowly?<br>Did you say…?<br>Do you mean…? |

1. Why is it important to make eye contact when you don't understand or don't hear?
2. What else can you say when you don't hear or don't understand?
3. When is it appropriate to use the less formal choices?

**E** Work with a partner. Take turns reading the sentences with nonsense words and asking for clarification.

A: *Do we have to fork list?*

B: *What was that?*

A: *Do we have to report this?*

**F** Have a staff conversation. Use the OSHA laws in B.

1. Work with a group. Take turns asking and answering questions.
2. Talk about what each law means for workers.

A: *Did you know that the law says that employers must …?*

B: *No, I didn't. What does that mean?*

A: *Well, if you think your workplace isn't safe, you can …*

**A** Work with a team. Write at least six sentences about the construction site. Use *should have* or *shouldn't have*.

*Amy should have checked the ladder before she used it.*

*Amy should not have used the ladder before she checked it.*

**B** Work with your team. Decide which sentences are closest in meaning. Circle *a* or *b*.

1. It's really important to use caution at a construction site.

   a. You must be careful at a construction site.

   b. You must not be careful at a construction site.

2. You don't have to wear a hard hat when you're in the construction office.

   a. You've got to wear a hard hat when you're in the construction office.

   b. It isn't necessary to wear a hard hat when you're in the construction office.

3. Put equipment away when you are done with it.

   a. You don't have to leave equipment around.

   b. You must not leave equipment around.

4. Do not ignore hazards or you could fall.

   a. To prevent falls, you must ignore hazards.

   b. To prevent falls, you must not ignore hazards.

5. All employees must report safety hazards.

   a. Employees have to report safety hazards.

   b. Employees don't have to report safety hazards.

6. If you follow the safety rules, you probably won't have an accident.

   a. You usually don't have to worry about accidents if you follow the safety rules.

   b. You have to worry about accidents if you follow the safety rules.

**C** Work with your class. Write a paragraph about the picture.

**D Work in a team. Follow the steps below to complete the task.**

1. Assign team roles: manager, director, actors.

2. Choose a problem from the list, or a different type of weather emergency that could happen in your community.

3. Write a conversation among family members to make an emergency plan.

4. Talk about what you have to do, what you don't have to do, and what you must not do.

5. Rehearse your conversation. Act it out for the class.

| Weather Emergencies |
| --- |
| • hurricane |
| • flood |
| • tornado |
| • snowstorm |
| • earthquake |

**E Interview three classmates. Write their answers.**

1. What is the most dangerous or unsafe situation you've ever seen? Did you report it? If you did, what happened?

2. Is it easy for you to report a dangerous or unsafe situation? Why or why not?

3. What are some things people should take with them if they have to evacuate their homes? What are some things they should not take?

**F Report your results for E to the class.**

## PROBLEM SOLVING

2-12

**A Listen and read about Mario.**

Mario works in a factory. He's worked there for a few months. The factory has a good safety-training program. Every employee is required to take a class and learn about keeping the workplace safe. Mario's co-workers follow the safety rules, but Mario has noticed one unsafe practice at his workplace. Some of the emergency exits are locked, even though a big sign on the door says, "This door must be unlocked at all times during work hours." Mario thinks that the emergency exits should be unlocked, but he doesn't know what to do.

**B Work with your classmates. Respond to the prompts.**

1. Identify Mario's problem.

2. Make a list of possible solutions Mario could try. For each solution, discuss the possible consequences.

# 6 Getting Ahead

## LESSON 1 VOCABULARY

## 1 Identify interpersonal skills

**A Collaborate with your classmates to complete each task.**

1. Brainstorm soft skills you have learned about.

2. Identify soft skills that you think are easier to do in English, and soft skills that are harder to do in English. State and discuss your reasons.

**B Work with a partner. Mark the chart.**

| Vocabulary | I know it | My partner knows it | We need to learn it |
|---|---|---|---|
| a. ask for clarification | | | |
| b. manage conflict | | | |
| c. solve problems | | | |
| d. give feedback | | | |
| e. resolve disagreements | | | |
| f. work on a team | | | |
| g. make suggestions | | | |
| h. respond to feedback | | | |

**C Check with your class. Look up the words nobody knows.**

**D Match each statement with the vocabulary from 1B.**

1. Marta doesn't like it when her young sons argue. She tries to __b__ by asking them to stop and giving them something else to do.

2. Marta can usually get her sons to stop arguing when they disagree; she has learned to _____ between them.

3. Marta likes to try to give people ideas that might help them. She likes to _____ .

4. Finding solutions in difficult situations is one of Marta's skills. She likes to _____ .

5. When Marta doesn't understand something at work, she knows she should _____ .

6. Marta likes working with her friends on community projects. She enjoys it when they _____ .

7. Marta's boss lets her know how she is doing at work. He believes a supervisor should _____ to employees.

8. Marta tries to follow her boss's advice. She knows it's important to _____ .

 **E Listen for information about interpersonal skills. Check your work in 1D.**

2-13

## 2 Learn about personal qualities

**A** Look at the employee evaluation. Complete the sentences. Use the words from the evaluation.

### EMPLOYEE EVALUATION FOR: AYANA ABEB

| Section 1: Personal Qualities | | |
|---|---|---|
| Employee is: | Rating* | Comments |
| reliable | 4 | Is always on time: completes all work |
| responsible | 4 | Works well without supervision |
| flexible | 2 | Sometimes has difficulty making changes |
| honest | 4 | Tells the truth and follows company rules |
| independent | 3 | Can work alone, but does best work on a team |
| tolerant | 4 | Works well with everyone; listens to others' ideas |

1. Ayana is ____reliable____ . I know she'll be here every day.
2. You can believe everything she says. She's very _____ .
3. She doesn't like to make changes. She needs to be more _____ .
4. She's a good team player, but she is also _____ .
5. She works hard when the supervisor isn't there. She's _____ .
6. She works well with everyone. She's _____ .

**B** Work with a partner. Practice talking about Ayana. Use the words in 2A.

*The supervisor thinks that Ayana is always reliable. She is on time and completes all her work.*

**C** Conduct research with a team. Survey your classmates to report on the questions.

1. When you work on a team, which interpersonal skills and personal qualities are the most important? Why?
2. Which skills and qualities are most important in a family? In a class?

**D** Report the results of your research.

*Our team thinks that...*

*Most of us think that...*

---

## ▶▶ TEST YOURSELF

Work with a partner. Take turns reading and responding to the prompts in 1D.

**Partner A:** Read prompts 1–4. Partner B Listen and write the vocabulary words.
**Partner B:** Read prompts 5–8. Partner A: Listen and write the vocabulary words.

# 1 Prepare to write

**A Look at the memo. Read the *To, From,* and *RE* lines. Talk about the questions with your class.**

1. What is the relationship between Ayana and Mr. Roberts? Why do you think so?

2. What do you think Ayana will talk about in the memo?

**B Listen and read the memo.**

2-14

To:      Mr. Roberts
From:   Ayana Abeb
RE:       Progress report

I would like to update you on my progress with the new office procedures we discussed at our meeting last month.

The new software for making patient appointments online has arrived and been installed. I am training all of the medical assistants to use the program. Three of the assistants have been trained; I still need to train the part-time weekend assistants. I hope to do that by the end of this month.

I have also been working on our scheduling system for the medical assistants. I have made some progress, but I would like to get everyone's input and opinions before I finalize the system. I expect to finish next week.

I would like to work on updating our system for entering patient information into medical records. I think that we need to make some changes. If you approve, I will take the initiative on this and give you some recommendations for changes.

I appreciate your feedback. Please let me know if you have any questions.

> **WRITER'S NOTE**
>
> A workplace memo includes *To, From,* and *RE* (subject) lines.
>
> Do not indent paragraphs in a memo or business letter.

**C Study the memo. Answer the questions.**

1. Paragraph 1: Why is Ayana writing this memo?

2. Paragraphs 2 and 3: What has Ayana finished? What does she still have to do?

3. Paragraph 4: What is Ayana proposing?

4. Paragraph 5: What is Ayana doing in this paragraph? Why?

## 2 Plan and write

**A** Talk about the questions with your class. Take notes.

1. Choose a topic you or your classmates have made progress on in your class. What progress have you made?

2. What do you still need to do?

**B** Write a progress report in memo format. Use the model memo in 1B and your answers to the questions in 2A.

```
○ ○ ○
To:
From:
Date:
RE:
I would like…
I have/I have been…
I hope to/I expect to…
I would like to work on…
I appreciate…
```

## 3 Get feedback and revise

**A** Use the editing checklist to review your writing. Check (✓) the true sentences.

☐ I explained what I have done.

☐ I described what I still need to do.

☐ I took initiative or made a suggestion.

☐ I used proper format for a memo.

**B** Exchange memos with a partner. Read and comment on your partner's work.

1. Point out sentences that you think are well written.

   *Your second paragraph explains your reasons well.*

   *Your offer to help is very clear.*

2. Give feedback about the email. Check your understanding.

   *I'm not sure I understand this sentence.*

   *I think you need to _____ here.*

**C** Use the checklist and your partner's feedback to revise your writing.

---

## ▶▶ TEST YOURSELF

Complete the following sentences. Share your responses with your teacher.

1. After this writing lesson, I can…
2. I need more help with…

# 1 Use adjective clauses

## A Read the conversation. Answer the questions below.

**Manager:** Here's your evaluation, Alonso. You're doing a great job.

**Alonso:** Thank you for saying so.

**Manager:** There's just one skill that needs work. Please try to make better eye contact with the customers who sit at your tables.

**Alonso:** OK, I will.

1. How many skills does Alonso need to work on?

2. What should he work on?

3. Which customers is the manager talking about?

## B Study the chart. Underline the adjective clauses in the conversation in 1A.

| Adjective clauses after main clauses | | |
|---|---|---|
| **Main clause** | **Adjective clause** | |
| There is one skill | which that | needs work. |
| Please greet the customers | who that | sit at your tables. |

**GRAMMAR NOTE**

Use adjective clauses to give more information:
*Alonso should greet the customers.*
**A:** *Which customers should Alonso greet?*
**B:** *Alonso should greet the customers who sit at his tables.*

## C Look at your answers to the questions in 1A. Complete the statements below.

**Language connection:** Ways to use adjective clauses

Use adjective clauses to give more information about an _____
(noun/adjective)
in the _____ clause of a sentence. Use *which* or _____
(main/adjective)                                                    (that/who)
when the adjective clause describes a thing. Use _____ or *that*
(who/which)
when the adjective clause describes a person.

**D** Combine the sentences with adjective clauses. Use *which* or *who*.

1. The manager made a suggestion. The suggestion helped Alonso.
   _The manager made a suggestion which helped Alonso._

2. Alonso has learned many skills. The skills are important in his job.

3. He always remembers the customers. The customers sit at his tables.

4. He is getting better at solving problems. Problems happen in the kitchen.

**E** Work in a team. Edit the sentences. Write the corrected sentence.

1. Tyra's manager gave her feedback *who* helped her.

2. He wants her to work on managing conflict with some of the people *which* work with her.

3. Tyra is happy to work on a skill *who* will help her and her team.

4. Her manager knows that Tyra is tolerant of people *which* don't share her opinions.

## 2 Use adjective clauses inside main clauses

**A** Study the chart. Combine the sentences below with adjective clauses. Two answers are possible for each.

| Adjective clauses inside main clauses | | | |
|---|---|---|---|
| Main clause / Adjective clause | | | |
| The manager | who / that | did Alonso's evaluation | made a suggestion |
| The skills | which / that | he learned on the job | helped him get a promotion. |

1. The manager was very happy. She had hired Alonso.
   _The manager who/that had hired Alonso was very happy._

2. The suggestion was about making eye contact. It helped Alonso.

3. The job opening was just filled. It was listed at the career center.

4. The woman quit after two days. She was hired last week.

**B** Complete the sentences with adjective clauses. Use your own ideas. Compare your opinions with a partner.

1. A company _____ is a good place to work.

2. People _____ are good employees.

3. A manager _____ is a good person to work for.

4. A person _____ is not a good manager.

5. A company _____ is not a good place to work.

6. People _____ are the best co-workers.

# 3 Use adjective clauses with *whose*

**A** Study the chart. Who are Mr. and Mrs. Lopez?

| Adjective clauses with *whose* | |
| --- | --- |
| **Main clause** | **Adjective clause** |
| Ms. Bell is the clerk | whose office is next to the cafe. |
| Mr. and Mrs. Lopez are the people | whose son works here. |

> **GRAMMAR NOTE**
>
> Adjective clauses with *whose* show who something belongs to.

**B** Work with a partner. Ask questions with *Who is …?* Combine the sentences with *whose* in your answer.

1. Margaret is one of the team leaders. Her feedback is the most helpful.

   **A:** *Who is Margaret?*      **B:** *She's the team leader whose feedback is the most helpful.*

2. Mr. Edwards is one of the teachers. His class is really popular.

3. Natasha and Jim are the employees. Their wedding was this weekend.

4. Julia is one of the students. Her mother lived in Italy last year.

5. Sima is one of our co-workers. She always tries to help everyone.

# 4 Building conversation skills

**A** Look at the picture and the conversation in 4B. What is the purpose of the conversation? How do you know?

🔊 2-19 **B** Listen to the sample conversation. How will Lu find Ms. Bell's office?

**A:** Hey, Lu! You look upset. What's wrong?

**B:** There's a big problem with my automatic deposit. Who do I see about it?

**A:** Oh, sorry to hear it. Go see Ms. Bell. She's the one whose office is so messy—papers are everywhere.

**B:** Oh, right, Ms. Bell is the person who takes care of payroll problems. OK, thanks, Nur.

> **IN OTHER WORDS…**
>
> Asking for information
> *Who do I see about…?*
> *Who do I talk to?*
> *How can I find out…?*
> *What do I do about…?*

**C** Role-play the situation below.

| Talk about | Roles | Instructions | Remember |
| --- | --- | --- | --- |
| Discussing how to get help with a problem | Classmate 1 | Your class schedule is wrong. Ask your classmate for information. Thank your classmate. | Use key phrases from 4B<br>Ask for information |
| | Classmate 2 | Tell your classmate to see Mr. Ang, the advisor. He takes care of schedule problems. | |

## 5 Focus on listening for details

**A** Brainstorm reasons customers and employees contact a company.

**B** Prepare to listen. Look at the web page. Predict what you will hear.

**(2-20)** **C** Listen to the automated phone menu. Number the offices in the order you hear them.

| _____ Business Services | _____ Main Office | _____ Human Resources |
| _____ Customer Service | _1_ Sales and Service | _____ Warehouse |

**(2-20)** **D** Listen again. Complete the phone directory for Martinez Electronics. Compare your answers with a partner.

| Office | Extension | Office | Extension |
|--------|-----------|--------|-----------|
| Business Services | | Main Office | |
| Customer Service | | Sales and Service | 111 |
| Human Resources | | Warehouse | |

## 6 Discuss

**A** Work with a group to make a chart. List actions and words you can use to demonstrate each interpersonal skill.

- work on a team
- make a suggestion
- give feedback
- ask for clarification
- respond to feedback

**B** Report the results of your discussion to the class.

*You can show that you are good at working on a team by asking for others' opinions.*

---

## ▶▶ TEST YOURSELF

Assess your participation in the group and class discussions. Today I was able to…

- ☐ listen effectively
- ☐ use language to demonstrate interpersonal skills
- ☐ speak accurately
- ☐ ask questions

## 3 Talk it over

**A** Look at the graph and read the note. Complete the sentences and answer the questions.

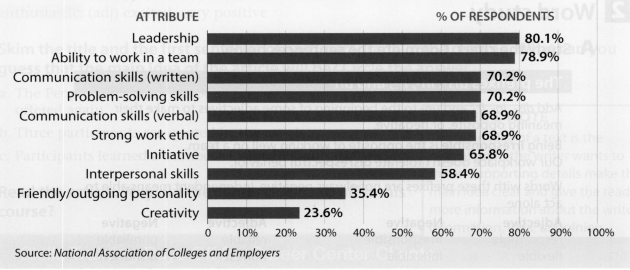

### Attributes employers are looking for

Employers often say that they can train employees in 'hard' job skills, like technical skills or skills specific to the job, as long as the employees have good interpersonal skills and personal qualities. In this survey, 60% of employers said they were looking for technical skills, and 55% of employers said that they were looking for computer skills. Leadership and other 'soft' skills were much more important to these employers.

**Attributes employers seek on a candidate's resume; 2015 survey of 200 employers**

| ATTRIBUTE | % OF RESPONDENTS |
|---|---|
| Leadership | 80.1% |
| Ability to work in a team | 78.9% |
| Communication skills (written) | 70.2% |
| Problem-solving skills | 70.2% |
| Communication skills (verbal) | 68.9% |
| Strong work ethic | 68.9% |
| Initiative | 65.8% |
| Interpersonal skills | 58.4% |
| Friendly/outgoing personality | 35.4% |
| Creativity | 23.6% |

Source: *National Association of Colleges and Employers*

1. Employers considered written communication skills and _____ equally important.

2. _____ was considered the least important skill.

3. About 1 out of _____ employers were looking for employees who were friendly.

4. Leadership skills were 1st on the list; computer skills were _____ .

5. Which attributes were less important than technical skills? _____

6. _____ employers said they were looking for leadership skills.

**B** Imagine you own a small business. What skills are important to you when you hire an employee? Rank the skills from #1 (most important) to #5 (least important).

1. ability to work individually _____    4. communication skills in writing _____

2. ability to work on a team _____    5. communication skills in speaking _____

3. computer skills _____

**C** Talk about your answers with your classmates.

---

 BRING IT TO LIFE

Search online. What skills do people in diverse groups need to live and work together?

**A** Listen to the supervisors' conversation. What are they discussing?

2-21

**B** Listen to the conversation again. Then put a check next to the qualities, skills, or experience each person has.

2-21

**Ana**

_____ responsible

_____ quiet

_____ flexible

**David**

_____ quiet

_____ makes suggestions

_____ good listener

**Tina**

_____ solves problems

_____ reliable

_____ had diversity training

**C** Listen again. Which employee do you think the supervisors prefer so far? Why do you think so? Tell a partner your ideas.

2-21

**D** Read the chart. Discuss the questions below with your class.

| When you want to show that you are listening actively, you can | |
| --- | --- |
| **Do this** | **Say this** |
| • Lean forward | Really? |
| • Nod your head slowly | Uh-huh |
| • Make eye contact | Go on… |
| • Tilt your head to one side | Oh! |
| • Take notes [in a meeting or in class] | Hmmmm.. |
| • Avoid interrupting | |

1. What message does it send if you lean toward a speaker?

2. What else can you say to encourage a speaker to continue?

3. When is it appropriate to take notes when someone is speaking?

**E** Work with a partner. Talk about the employees in B. Use the notes.

**Ana:**   _reliable; responsible; quiet. Needs communication skills training._

**David:**   _makes suggestions; loud; good at speaking, not at listening. Give feedback._

**Tina:**   _solves problems; good at teamwork; had diversity training. Consider for promotion._

**F** Have a supervisors' meeting.

1. Work with a group to make a list of three employees you are considering for a promotion. Write qualities for each one.

2. Take turns bringing up the employees and considering their qualities, skills, and experience. Use the ideas from your list and from this page.

**A:** _What do you think about…?_

**B:** _Well, she's very…and…_

**A:** _Go on…_

**B:** _Well, she's very…and…_

**A:** _Go on…_

**A** Work with a team. Look at the picture and decide who the employees are. Write questions and answers based on your decisions.

new employee
janitor
nursing supervisor
physical therapy aide
social worker
dietician
receptionist
physical therapist

*Which one is the new employee? He's the one who is wearing the green scrubs.*

**B** Assign each team member one or more of the pairs of sentences below. Take turns combining the sentences using adjective clauses with *who, which, that,* or *whose.* Tell your teammates if you agree or disagree with their choice and say why.

1. Disagreements can cause big problems on the job. The disagreements aren't resolved.
    <u>Disagreements that aren't resolved can cause big problems on the job.</u>

2. Mr. Freeman is the art therapist. His patients drew the pictures in the hall.

3. Emilio is good at giving feedback. It helps employees.

4. The team won $100. The team solved the problem.

5. Sarah's background is in engineering. Sarah helped the team win.

6. I like working with people. People can resolve disagreements.

7. Sean is the physical therapy aide. His patients complained.

8. Mr. Diaz was the supervisor. His suggestions really helped me.

9. Mrs. Tanaka was the dietician. Her meals were very creative.

10. Emilio supervises 10 employees. The 10 employees work well together.

**C** Work with your class. Write a paragraph about the picture. Use *who, that, whose,* and *which.*

**D** Work in a team. Follow the steps below to complete the task.

• an excellent leader
• a good politician
• a good supervisor

1. Assign team roles: manager, writer, editor, presenter.

2. Identify the characteristics or attributes of one of the types of people.

3. Decide on someone you all know who has the characteristics you've named.

4. Collaborate on a paragraph describing this person and his or her attributes, but do not put his or her name in the paragraph.

5. Read your paragraph to the class. Have the class guess who you are describing.

**E** Interview three classmates. Write their answers.

1. Do you know someone who gets along with everyone? Who is it? How does he/she do it?

2. Which interpersonal skill would you like to develop? Why?

3. What are three things that every manager (or teacher or parent) should do to help employees/students/children? Why?

**F** Report your results for Exercise E, #2 to the class. What percent of your class gave each answer? Make a graph with your class results.

## PROBLEM SOLVING AT HOME

2-22

**A** Listen and read about Lana.

Lana has just gotten a promotion at work. She is a team manager for a group of six employees. Lana really wants to be a success in her new job, but her group isn't really a team. Two of the people in her group don't like each other and argue a lot. There is one team member who talks all the time and another one who never says a word. The team members are from six different countries, and two of the countries they come from don't get along. Lana doesn't know what to do.

**B** Work with your classmates. Respond to the prompts.

1. Identify Lana's problem.

2. Make a list of possible solutions Lana could try.

3. Role-play a conversation between Lana and a friend. Offer advice.

# Making Ends Meet

**A LOOK AT**
- Finance and budgeting
- Present unreal conditionals
- Building consensus at work

## LESSON **1** VOCABULARY

### **1** Identify vocabulary for personal finance and banking

**A** Collaborate with your classmates. Look at the picture, read the text, and answer the questions.

1. What are some services that banks and credit unions offer?

2. Are you good at managing money? What money skills do you have?

**Financial Literacy Workshop**

**May 2, 7 p.m.**

**Take control of your future!**

- Set and reach your financial goals
- Learn to maximize your assets and minimize debts
- How to manage credit
- Borrowing money: how to get and pay back loans
- How to protect your identity and avoid scams

**B** Use context clues. What do you think the bold words in the workshop flyer mean? How do you know? Compare your ideas with a partner.

**C** Complete the statements with the words from the picture. Then, listen and check your work.
2-23

Roberto and Julia…

1. have _____ of about $6,500, and have _____ of about $4,000.

2. have been thinking about getting a _____ to buy a house.

3. would need an _____ if they wanted to buy a car.

4. The _____ for auto loans is 3.3% right now.

**D** Listen again. What kinds of loans are Roberto and Julia thinking about?
2-23

**E** Ask and answer the questions with your partner.

1. What types of accounts and loans do banks offer?

2. What types of assets and debts do people often have?

3. What kinds of insurance do people often have?

## 2 Learn about budgeting

### A Look at Julia and Roberto's budget. Match the words with their definitions.

| Our budget | | | Per month | |
|---|---|---|---|---|
| Net income | Julia's salary | | $2,400 | $3,300 remaining after rent |
| | Roberto's salary | | $2,000 | |
| Expenses | Fixed expenses | Rent | $1,100 | |
| | | Car insurance premium | $200 | |
| | | Student loans | $300 | |
| | Variable expenses | Food | $300 | $1,200 per month |
| | | Utilities | $200 | |
| | | Gas | $200 | |
| | | Miscellaneous (clothes, gifts, eating out, etc.) | $400 | |

_d_ 1. fixed expenses

____ 2. variable expenses

____ 3. income

____ 4. mortgage payment

____ 5. premium

____ 6. miscellaneous

a. money from a job or other sources

b. money you pay for insurance

c. things that cost a different amount each month

d. things that cost the same each month

e. things that don't fit in any other category

f. money you pay for a home loan

### B Work with a partner. Practice the conversation. Use the words and amounts in 2A.

A: How much did they pay for utilities last month?

B: They paid $200! Wow! That seems like a lot.

### C Conduct research with a team. Look at websites and/or survey your classmates in order to report on the questions below.

1. What are the benefits of household budgets?

2. How can people learn about financial literacy?

### D Report the results of your research.

_Our team found that _____ ._

_People can learn about financial literacy _____ ._

## ▶▶ TEST YOURSELF

Work with a partner. Take turns reading and responding to the prompts in 2A.

**Partner A:** Read prompts 1–3. Partner B: Listen and write the vocabulary words.
**Partner B:** Read prompts 4–6. Partner A: Listen and write the vocabulary words.

## 1 Prepare to write

**A** Read the essay prompt, the essay title, and the last paragraph of the essay. Talk about the questions with your class.

1. What are some ways that having or not having money affects people's lives?

2. In your opinion, do people pay too much attention to money? Explain your answer.

 **B** Listen and read the essay.

2-24

> ### Topic
>
> Tell why you agree or disagree with this statement: "Money can't buy happiness." Limit your essay to 125 words.
>
> ---
>
> > **Money Can't Buy Happiness**
> > by Edwin Thomas
> >
> > Money is important. People who have money have more comfortable lives than people who don't. They have more free time, more security, and more flexibility. Most people would probably say that they would like to have more money. However, many of these people would probably also agree that money can't buy happiness.
> >
> > Happiness is a feeling. It can come from being with your family or friends, from good news, from kind words, or from a happy event. Money can help make good things happen, but it can't buy time, friends, or love. Money can only buy things.
> >
> > People can find happiness in everyday life and in other people. Being financially secure can certainly help, but the old saying is still true: "Money can't buy happiness."

**WRITER'S NOTE**

Formal essays respond to a prompt (a topic or question). They usually have several paragraphs: one to introduce the topic, one or more to give details, and one to summarize. Formal essays don't usually use the first person pronoun *I* or statements like *I think*… or *In my opinion*.

**C** Study the essay. Answer the questions.

1. According to Edwin, what four things can money buy?

   _____

2. What does he think most people want?

   _____

3. According to Edwin, what things bring happiness?

   _____

## 2 Plan and write

**A** **Talk about the questions with your class. Take notes.**

1. Name two famous people who have a lot of money. What do you think their lives are like?

2. What have these people done to change the world or to help others?

3. Name someone who has changed the world. Did the person use money to make changes?

**B** **Write an essay about money. Use the model essay in 1B and your answers to the questions in 2A.**

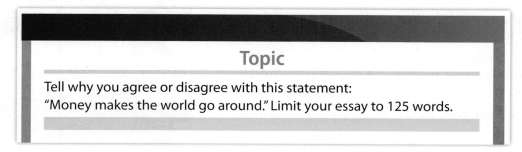

### Topic

Tell why you agree or disagree with this statement:
"Money makes the world go around." Limit your essay to 125 words.

## 3 Get feedback and revise

**A** **Use the editing checklist to review your writing. Check (✔) the true sentences.**

☐ I responded to the topic in the prompt.

☐ I gave my opinions without using *I*.

☐ I used commas between items in lists.

☐ My essay is not more than 125 words.

**B** **Exchange essays with a partner. Read and comment on your partner's work.**

1. Point out the sentences that you think are well written.

   *Your sentence, "However, most people …" shows that you have thought about both sides of the question.*

   *Your last paragraph summarizes your ideas clearly.*

2. Give feedback about the essay. Check your understanding.

   *I'm not sure I understand this sentence.*

   *I think you need _____ here.*

**C** **Use the checklist and your partner's feedback to revise your writing.**

---

### ▶▶TEST YOURSELF

Complete the following sentences. Share your responses with your teacher.

1. After this writing lesson, I can…
2. I need more help with…

## **1** Use present unreal conditional statements

**A** Read the conversation. Answer the questions below.

> **Isabel:** If I go out for lunch, will you go with me?
>
> **Molly:** Thanks, but I brought my lunch. I'm trying to save money.
>
> **Isabel:** I know. If I didn't eat in the cafe every day, I'd save about $40 a week.
>
> **Molly:** I'm saving for college—that's my dream. If I had enough money, I'd start today. But I don't, so I'm watching my expenses.
>
> **Isabel:** Good for you, Molly! Go get your dream.

1. What does Isabel want Molly to do at lunchtime?

2. Can Molly go to college right now?

3. How much does Isabel spend on lunch every week?

4. Why is Molly watching her expenses?

**B** Study the charts. Underline the present unreal conditional statements in the conversation in 1A.

| Present unreal conditional statements | |
|---|---|
| **If clause** | **Main clause** |
| **If** Molly **had** enough money, | she **could start** college now. |
| **If** she **had** enough money now, | she **wouldn't have to wait**. |
| **If** Isabel **didn't eat** in the cafe, | she **would save** money. |

**GRAMMAR NOTE**

In unreal conditionals, the *if* clause can also come after the main clause, and there is no comma:
*Molly could start college right now if she had enough money.*

**C** Look at your answers to the questions in 1A. Complete the statements below.

> **Language connection:** Using present unreal conditional statements
>
> We can use present unreal conditional statements to talk about situations that are
>
> _____ or _____. We use the _____ clause to talk about an unreal
>   (true/not true)   (possible/not possible)   (if/main)
>
> condition, and the _____ clause to talk about what would happen if the condition were
>   (if/main)
>
> true. The verb in the *if* clause is in the _____ tense form.
>   (simple present/simple past)

**D** Complete the sentences to make present unreal conditional statements. Use the verbs in parentheses.

1. It <u>would be</u> easier for Isabel to save money if she <u>limited</u> her spending. (be, limit)

2. If she _____ the bus, she _____ a lot of money on gas. (take, save)

3. If she _____ a savings account, it _____ easier to save her money. (open, be)

4. Isabel _____ $160 a month if she _____ her lunch. (save, bring)

**E** Work in a team. Edit the sentences. Write the corrected sentence.

1. Sunny would spend less money if she shops at less expensive stores.

   _____

2. If she did that, she will be able to pay back her loan more quickly.

   _____

3. She can start this weekend if she wanted to.

   _____

## 2  Use present unreal conditional questions

**A** Study the chart. Circle the correct words in the sentences below.

| Present unreal conditional questions | |
|---|---|
| **Yes/No questions and short answers** | |
| **A:** Could Molly go to college if she didn't have to work? <br> **B:** Yes, she could. | **A:** If your son wanted a credit card, would you give him one? <br> **B:** No, I wouldn't. |
| **Information questions** | |
| **A:** What would Molly do if she had enough money? <br> **B:** She would go to college. | **A:** If you could live anywhere, where would you live? <br> **B:** I'd live in Hawaii. |
| **GRAMMAR NOTE** | |
| Don't use contracted forms (*she'd, he'd,* etc.) in affirmative short answers. | |

1. Who would you call if you ( have / had ) a money emergency?

2. Would he save a lot of money if he ( walked / would walk ) to work?

**B** Complete the questions and answers. Use the verbs in parentheses.

1. **A:** If you <u>didn't need</u> money, <u>would</u> you <u>keep</u> your second job? (not need, keep)

   **B:** Yes, I <u>would</u> . I like that job.

2. **A:** If you _____ a car, _____ you _____ to work? (have, drive)

   **B:** No, I _____ . Gas is too expensive.

3. **A:** How much money _____ she _____ if she _____ at expensive stores? (can save, not shop)

   **B:** She _____ fifty or sixty dollars a month. (save)

4. **A:** What _____ you _____ first if you _____ to buy a house? (do, want)

   **B:** I _____ a budget and stick to it! (make)

## 3 Listen for the present unreal conditionals to determine the meaning

🔊 2-25 **Listen to the conversations. Circle the correct statement.**

1. a. She has a credit card.

   b. She has to carry cash.

2. a. He uses a credit card.

   b. He doesn't use a credit card.

3. a. She has to study.

   b. She watches a movie every night.

4. a. He has to study.

   b. He would like to watch a movie every night.

## 4 Use present unreal conditionals to talk about your ideas

**A** Use present unreal conditionals to complete the questions.

1. If you ___had___ $100 to spend on your classroom or school, how <u>would you spend</u> it?
   (have, spend)

2. What _____ if you _____ $1,000 to spend on your classroom or school? Why?
   (do, have)

3. If you _____ one change in your school, what _____? (can make, change)

**B** Work with a partner. Write two more questions.

1. If you were _____ ?

2. What would you do if you could _____ ?

**C** Work in a team. Ask and answer the questions in 4A and 4B. Take notes on your teammates' responses.

Ella: *If you had $100 to spend on our classroom, how would you spend it?*

Tai: *I would buy a bus pass for every student.*

Ella: *Why would you do that?*

Tai: *Well, I'd do it because…*

▶▶ **TEST YOURSELF**

Close your book. Refer to your notes and write six sentences using the information you learned about your classmates. Use present unreal conditionals.

*If Tai had $ 200 to spend on our class, she would buy bus passes for us because the bus is expensive and passes are a good way to save. . . .*

## 1 Learn ways to negotiate and compromise on a budget

🔊 2-26 **A** **Listen to the conversation. What are Julia and Roberto trying to do?**

🔊 2-26 **B** **Listen again for the answers. Compare answers with your partner.**

1. How much do Julia and Roberto agree to spend on groceries?
2. How do they decide on that amount?
3. What does each one agree to do to save more money?
4. What do you think *It's a deal* means?

🔊 2-27 **C** **Listen. Write the words Julia and Roberto use to negotiate and compromise.**

1. Let's compromise. _____ $250?
2. Well, _____ coffee at home and took it to work?
3. And _____ stopped buying lunch at work?

## 2 Practice your pronunciation

🔊 2-28 **A** **Listen to the sentences. Notice that the speakers pause at the commas.**

1. If you didn't buy coffee, we'd save a lot of money.
2. If we budgeted $250, we could still buy fresh fruit and vegetables.

🔊 2-29 **B** **Note the commas in these sentences. Say the sentences. Then listen and check the pauses.**

1. If we cut back our spending, we could save to buy a house.
2. Fresh fruit can be expensive, but it's worth it.
3. If you brought snacks to work, you wouldn't have to buy them from a machine.
4. If we bought a new car, we'd be in debt.
5. If we're careful, we'll be able to follow this budget.
6. Coffee places are expensive, so make your own coffee.

🔊 2-29 **C** **Listen again and repeat the sentences in 2B.**

## 3 Use present unreal conditionals with *be*

**A** Look at the picture. Is Jason's father giving him good advice?

**Present unreal conditionals with *be***

What would you do?

If I were you, I'd look for a newer car.

$5,000 2008

If his father weren't here, Jason would buy the car.

**GRAMMAR NOTE**

In formal speech with present unreal conditionals, use *were* for all people (*I, you, he, she,* etc.). *If I **were** you, I'd look for a newer car.*

**B** Check your understanding. Complete the sentences with *were* or *weren't*. Ask and answer the questions with a partner.

1. Jason would buy the car today if it __were__ cheaper.

2. If the car _____ so old, Jason's father would like it better.

3. Jason would be more comfortable if the salesman _____ listening.

4. If you _____ Jason, what would you do?

## 4 Building conversation skills

**A** Look at the picture and the conversation in 4B. What is the purpose of the conversation? How do you know?

**B** Listen to the sample conversation. Why is the woman going to contact Marisa?

2-30

**A:** We need to start here, at the back.

**B:** I agree. Let's have Tony start there and then come to the front.

**A:** Hmm. What if we had Petra help him? It's a big job.

**B:** OK; sounds good. But it would be better if Marisa were here too. We could use another set of hands.

**A:** OK. How about if I got Marisa here after lunch?

**B:** That would really help.

**A:** Great; it's a deal. Let's get started!

**IN OTHER WORDS...**

Make a suggestion to negotiate and compromise

*What if I* + (simple past verb)…?

*How about if you* + (simple past verb)…?

*How about we* + (simple present verb)…?

*Let's …*

**C** Role-play the situation below.

| Talk about | Roles | Instructions | Remember |
|---|---|---|---|
| Collaborating on a plan to get a job done | manager | You need to finish a big job today. Another employee could help move boxes. You could call a third employee in a few minutes. | Use key phrases from 4B<br><br>Negotiate and compromise |
| | team leader | One employee could start moving boxes to the truck. You would like another employee to come in early. You could use the help. | |

## 5 Focus on listening for details

### A Talk about the questions with a partner.

1. What advice would you give a friend who wants to save money?
2. What do you think *credit counseling* means?

### B Listen to the conversation. Answer the questions.

2-31

1. What is Ms. Sanchez's job?
2. What is Mr. Moreno's problem?

### C Listen again. Circle the correct answer.

2-31

1. Mr. Moreno pays _____ on his credit card each month.
   a. the total due
   b. the minimum payment
2. His total debt is about _____
   a. $5,000
   b. $15,000
3. He spends about $400 a month _____ .
   a. on eating dinner
   b. on food

4. If he followed Ms. Sanchez' suggestions, he'd save about _____ a year.
   a. $2,000
   b. $20,000
5. Ms. Sanchez thinks he should _____ .
   a. get a home loan
   b. get a low-interest loan
6. She also thinks that he should _____ .
   a. cut up his credit cards
   b. put his cards away for one year

## 6 Discuss

### A Work with a group. Read the question and collaborate to make a list. *What are the best ways to save money in your area?*

A: *I think shopping at the farmer's market saves money.*

B: *Can you say a little more about that? I thought it was expensive.*

### B Report the results of your discussion to the class.

*We think that the best ways to save money are …*

> **SPEAKING NOTE**
>
> **Ask for more detail**
> *What do you mean by "a lot of money"?*
> *Can you say a little more about how…?*
> *How would that work?*

---

## ▶▶ TEST YOURSELF

Assess your participation in the group and class discussions. Today I was able to…

☐ listen effectively      ☐ negotiate and compromise

☐ speak accurately      ☐ ask questions

## 3 Talk it over

**A** Look at the pie chart and read the note. Complete the sentences.

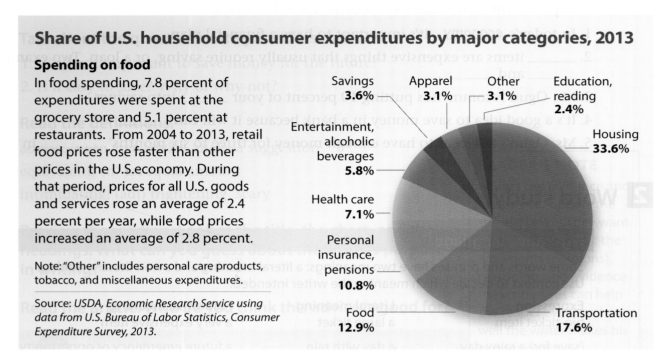

### Share of U.S. household consumer expenditures by major categories, 2013

**Spending on food**

In food spending, 7.8 percent of expenditures were spent at the grocery store and 5.1 percent at restaurants. From 2004 to 2013, retail food prices rose faster than other prices in the U.S.economy. During that period, prices for all U.S. goods and services rose an average of 2.4 percent per year, while food prices increased an average of 2.8 percent.

Note: "Other" includes personal care products, tobacco, and miscellaneous expenditures.

Source: *USDA, Economic Research Service using data from U.S. Bureau of Labor Statistics, Consumer Expenditure Survey, 2013.*

Savings 3.6%
Apparel 3.1%
Other 3.1%
Education, reading 2.4%
Housing 33.6%
Entertainment, alcoholic beverages 5.8%
Health care 7.1%
Personal insurance, pensions 10.8%
Food 12.9%
Transportation 17.6%

1. In 2013, American households spent the largest percentage of their money on _housing_ .

2. Americans spent the least money on _____ .

3. Housing, food and transportation together are about _____ percent of spending.

4. About 40 percent of Americans' food budgets was spent on food at _____ .

**B** Think about the questions. Write your notes in a chart like the one below.

| | Question 1 | Question 2 | Question 3 | Question 4 |
|---|---|---|---|---|
| My Ideas | | | | |
| | | | | |
| | | | | |

1. How did you learn about spending and saving money when you were a child?

2. Who do you think should teach children about money?

3. Should communities offer free financial literacy training to their members?

4. How have your feelings about money changed over the last ten years?

**C** Talk about your answers with your classmates.

---

 BRING IT TO LIFE

Look around your school. Brainstorm ways that your school could save money. Outline a plan with your classmates.

**A** Listen to the conversation. What are they discussing?
2-32

**B** Listen to the conversation again. Then put a check next to each problem that
2-32 is mentioned.

_____ they don't have a written budget     _____ they don't agree on expanding the business

_____ they don't know how much money     _____ their daughters don't want to work in the
they have                                  bakery any more

**C** Listen again. Complete the sentences. Discuss your answers with a partner.
2-32

1. Laila and Omar agree that they need _____ and _____ .

2. Omar would like to _____ , but Laila isn't really sure.

3. Before they meet again, Ms. Chang asks them to:

     a. _____       c. _____

     b. _____       d. _____

**D** Read the chart. Discuss the questions below with your class.

| When you want to build consensus, you can | |
|---|---|
| **Do this** | **Say this** |
| • Look at everyone in the group equally.<br>• Listen actively to each person. | Let's look at this [problem] again.<br>Some of us think… and some of us think…<br>Can we agree that …?<br>How can we make everyone happy?<br>I think we've reached a consensus. |

1. Why is it important to look at everyone equally?

2. What else can you do when you want to build consensus in a group?

**E** Have a business partners' meeting.

1. You are co-owners of a small business. Plan a company party for your employees. Some of you want to pay for the party as a thank-you to your employees, and some want to save money by having a potluck with everyone bringing food to share.

2. Make a list of the advantages and disadvantages of each idea.

3. Choose one person to run the meeting. Discuss ideas and suggestions. Come to a consensus.

A: *OK, what are our options? Who wants to go first?*

B: *I think that we should…because…*

C: *I'm not so sure. We have to think about…*

# TEAMWORK & LANGUAGE REVIEW

**A** **Work with a team. Take turns reading the information and voting on which statement is true.**

1. Ed would buy a car if he didn't have credit card debt.

   a. Ed has credit card debt.          b. Ed doesn't have credit card debt.

2. If Joan had to pay for her checks, she would change banks.

   a. Joan has to pay for her checks.          b. Joan doesn't have to pay for her checks.

3. If you didn't have a debit card, you'd have to write a check to get cash.

   a. You have a debit card.          b. You have to write a check to get cash.

4. If they didn't want a new car, they wouldn't have to take out a loan.

   a. They have to take out a loan.          b. They want a used car.

**B** **Work with your team. Use the verbs in parentheses and your own ideas to complete the conversation between Mr. and Mrs. Tan and the accounts manager who is explaining the account options.**

**Mrs. Tan:**  We need to save money. If we opened an account here, what would you give us?

**Manager:**  If (1) _____ (you/open) an account today, (2) _____ (I/give) an ATM card, and a free checkbook.

**Mr. Tan:**  OK, that sounds good.

**Mrs. Tan:**  Now, help us understand how this account works. For example, if (3) _____ (we/put) $ _____ in this account every _____, how much (4) _____ (we/have) by _____?

**Manager:**  If (5) _____ (you/deposit) $ _____ in the account, (6) _____ (you/earn) $ _____ in interest by _____.

**Mr. Tan:**  And what about checks? I don't like to use credit cards.

**Manager:**  If (7) _____ (you/keep) $ _____ in your account, your checks (8) _____ (be free).

**Mrs. Tan:**  If (9) _____ (we/open) a joint account, (10) _____ (we/get) two free _____ ?

**Manager:**  Of course!

**Mr. Tan:**  Then let's start the paperwork!

## C Work with a team. Follow the steps below to complete the task.

1. Assign team roles: writer, director, editor, actors.
2. Write a conversation between two people about their financial situation. Include goals and problems; reach a compromise.
3. Use the words from the list on the right and your own ideas.
4. Rehearse your conversation. Act it out for the class.

- goals
- assets
- debts
- loans
- financial advisor
- budget
- savings
- income
- expenses
- compromise
- need
- want

## D Interview three classmates. Write their answers.

1. Are you more often a spender or a saver?
2. What do you think motivates people (makes them want) to save money? Why?
3. If you could give everyone in this class one piece of advice about money, what would it be?

## E Report your results for Exercise D, #1 to the class. Make a pie chart with your class results.

# PROBLEM SOLVING

2-33

## A Listen and read about Lula.

Lula's best friend, Adele, has a money problem. Adele has a good job and she makes a good salary, but she isn't very careful with her money. For example, she likes nice clothes, and she often buys them. She always has lunch at a restaurant on workdays, and she eats dinner out several nights a week, too. When she buys groceries, she shops at an expensive supermarket because the food looks so good there. Adele is a generous person, and she often buys expensive gifts for her friends. Lula doesn't think Adele puts any money into savings, and she's worried about her.

## B Work with your classmates. Respond to the prompts.

1. Identify Lula's problem.
2. What would you do if you were Lula? Think of two or three possible solutions.
3. Discuss the possible consequences of each idea.

# 8 Satisfaction Guaranteed

## LESSON 1 VOCABULARY

## 1 Identify shopping vocabulary

**A** **Collaborate with your classmates to complete each task.**

1. Brainstorm places and ways to shop for things you need.
2. How do you buy food, clothes, and household items? Do you shop online? State and discuss your reasons.

**B** **Work with a partner. Mark the chart.**

| Vocabulary | I know it | My partner knows it | We need to learn it |
|---|---|---|---|
| a. as is | | | |
| b. catalog | | | |
| c. on clearance | | | |
| d. online store | | | |
| e. on sale | | | |
| f. thrift store | | | |
| g. shopping network | | | |
| h. yard sale | | | |

**C** **Check with your class. Look up the words nobody knows.**

**D** **Match each question with the vocabulary from 1B.**

__f__ 1. Where can you go to buy used clothes, furniture, and household items?

_____ 2. What is the name for a TV station that sells items you can order by phone?

_____ 3. What can you have if you want to sell items from your home?

_____ 4. What do we call items that have been reduced to the lowest possible price?

_____ 5. What is the name for a website you can order and buy items from?

_____ 6. What do you call a booklet with pictures of things that are for sale?

_____ 7. What do you call an item with a reduced price for a short time?

_____ 8. What do we call an item that is for sale at a reduced price because it is damaged?

 **E** **Listen for information about shopping. Check your work in 1D.**
2-34

## 2 Learn to describe purchase problems

**A** Look at the picture. Complete the customers' sentences.

RETURNS AND DEFECTIVE MERCHANDISE

SCRATCHED   FADED   DENTED   STAINED   TORN   DEFECTIVE

OUR GUARANTEE:

FULL REFUND ON ANY PURCHASE WITHIN 30 DAYS

Doesn't work

1. "One part of it is a lighter color. It's _faded_ ."
2. "It's _____ . The glass has a big mark on it."
3. "It's new, but it doesn't work. It's _____ ."
4. "Look—it's _____ . It looks like something hit it."
5. "This happened the first time I put it on. It's _____ ."
6. "It's _____ . It looks like there's coffee on it."

**B** Work with a partner. Practice the conversation. Use the words in 2A.

A: *Excuse me. I'd like to return this mirror. It's scratched.*

B: *Certainly. Would you like to exchange it, or would you like a refund?*

A: *…*

**C** Conduct research with a team. Look at websites and community newsletters, and/or survey your classmates in order to report on the questions below.

1. Which items are best to buy in person? Online? Over the phone? Why?
2. What are some possible problems with items you buy at yard sales, flea markets, or thrift stores? What can you do about these problems?

**D** Report the results of your research.

*Our team discovered that most of us like to buy _____ at _____ .*

*We agree that when you buy _____ , you should _____ .*

## ▶▶TEST YOURSELF

Work with a partner. Take turns reading and responding to the prompts in 1D.

**Partner A:** Read prompts 1–4. Partner B: Listen and write the vocabulary words.
**Partner B:** Read prompts 5–8. Partner A: Listen and write the vocabulary words.

## **1** Use adjectives ending in *-ed* and *-ing*

**A** Read the conversation. Answer the questions below.

> **Cho:** I got this new video game, and I'm really disappointed with it.
>
> **Todd:** You are? Why?
>
> **Cho:** Well, it was supposed to be exciting, but it's not. It's kind of boring.
>
> **Todd:** Can you return it?
>
> **Cho:** Just because I don't like it? I don't think so. If you're interested in it, you can have it.
>
> **Todd:** Uh…OK, thanks.

1. Does Cho like or dislike the video game? Why?
2. What did Cho think about the game before he got it?
3. What does he think about it now?
4. Do we know if Todd likes the game?

**B** Study the charts. Circle two examples of adjectives ending in *-ing* and two adjectives ending in *-ed* in the conversation in 1A.

| Adjectives ending in *-ed* and *-ing* | |
| --- | --- |
| **Adjectives ending in *-ed*** | **Adjectives ending in *-ing*** |
| Cho was **disappointed** with the game. | The game was **disappointing**. |
| We were **bored** with the movie. We left after 15 minutes. | The movie was really **boring**. |

**GRAMMAR NOTE**

- Adjectives ending in *-ed* describe a person's feelings: *Cho was **disappointed** because the game wasn't good.*
- Adjectives ending in *-ing* describe the cause of the feelings: *Cho was unhappy because the game wasn't **exciting**.*

**C** Look at your answers to the questions in 1A, and the chart in 1B. Complete the statements below.

> **Language connection:** Adjectives ending in *-ed* and *-ing*
>
> Adjectives ending in _____ usually describe a person's feelings. Adjectives that end in
>     (-ed/-ing)
> _____ usually describe the cause of a person's feelings. Adjectives ending in *-ing* are
> (-ed/-ing)
> usually used to describe _____ while adjectives ending in _____ usually, but
>     (people/things)                         (-ed/-ing)
> not always, are used to describe _____.
>     (people/things)

**D Circle the correct adjective.**

1. We were really ( boring / bored ) last night, so we watched a movie and ordered a pizza.
2. The pizza wasn't very good. I was ( disappointing / disappointed ).
3. The movie was ( confusing / confused ) at first. I couldn't understand it.
4. After about 30 minutes, though, the movie got much more ( exciting / excited ).

**E Work with your class. Circle the true statement.**

1. Sam didn't like his old job. He did the same thing every day.
   a. Sam was bored by his job.     b. Sam was boring.
2. Sam's new job is more interesting, and he likes it much better.
   a. Sam's new job is satisfying.     b. Sam's new job is satisfied.
3. Sam's new boss has a good sense of humor, and she's funny. Sam appreciates that.
   a. Sam's boss is amused.     b. Sam's boss is amusing.

## 2 Use adverbs of degree

**A Study the chart. Circle the correct words in the sentences below.**

**Adverbs of degree**

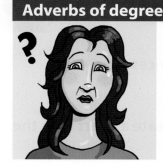   

I'm **a little** confused.  I'm **pretty** confused.  I'm **really** confused.  I'm **extremely**
I'm **somewhat**  I'm **fairly** confused.  I'm **very** confused.  confused.
confused.

1. The customer said he was never coming back. He was ( really / a little ) annoyed.
2. Don't throw your receipts away! It's ( extremely / fairly ) important to keep them.
3. I got this book on final clearance for 90% off, so it was ( very / fairly ) cheap.
4. The watch is in good condition. It's only ( a little / extremely ) scratched.

**B Complete the sentences with an adverb of degree or the word *not*. Compare your answers with a partner.**

1. I am _____ comfortable with shopping in stores in the U.S.
2. Returning items to the store is _____ easy for me.
3. Return policies and guarantees are _____ difficult for me to understand.
4. For me, ordering items online is _____ easy.
5. Shopping at yard sales and flea markets is _____ unusual in my country.

## 3 Listen for the adjectives to determine the meaning

2-36

**Listen to the speakers. Circle the correct response.**

1. a. Actually, it was a little disappointing.   b. Actually, it was a little disappointed.
2. a. Not really. I was pretty confused at first.   b. Not really. I was pretty confusing at first.
3. a. I thought it was a little bored.   b. I thought it was a little boring.
4. a. They thought I was excited.   b. They thought it was exciting.
5. a. No, I didn't. That's surprising.   b. No, I didn't. He's surprising.
6. a. No, thanks. I'm really not interesting.   b. No, thanks. I'm really not interested.

## 4 Use adjectives ending in -ed and -ing and adverbs of degree to talk about your life experience

**A  Think about each of the experiences below.**

1. a time when you did something really exciting
2. a time when something interesting happened to you
3. a time when you were really bored
4. a time when something confusing happened. How confusing was it?

**B  Work with a partner. Describe one or more of the experiences from 4A.**

*I did something really exciting when I was 15. I...*

**C  Work in a team. Talk about your partner's experiences. Create a chart with the information.**

*Angela did something really exciting when she was 15.*
*She...*

| Name | exciting | interesting | | |
|---|---|---|---|---|
| | | | | |
| | | | | |

---

## ▶▶ TEST YOURSELF

Close your book. Refer to your chart and write six sentences using the information you learned about your classmates. Use adjectives ending in -ed and -ing and adverbs of degree.

*Something very interesting happened to Kai at work last week. He was...*

# 1 Learn ways to report problems with services

🔊 2-37 **A** Listen to the conversation. What does Tara say caused the problem?

🔊 2-37 **B** Listen again for the answers. Compare answers with your partner.

1. What problems is Mr. Andrews calling to report?
2. Does Tara know when the problems will be fixed?
3. What does Tara offer to tell Mr. Andrews about at the end of the conversation?

🔊 2-38 **C** Listen. Write the words Mr. Andrews uses to report and ask about the problems.

1. Hello, Tara. _____ with my cable service.
2. Well, _____ I can't get cable TV, and the Internet is down too.
3. It's been out since this morning. _____ ?

# 2 Practice your pronunciation

🔊 2-39 **A** Read the chart. Then listen to the pronunciation. Notice how the speakers link the words.

| Linked consonants and vowels | | |
| --- | --- | --- |
| When one word ends in a consonant sound and the next word begins with a vowel sound, the two words are often connected, or linked, in speaking | | |
| I'm afraid not. | How can I help you? | Thanks anyway. |

🔊 2-40 **B** Listen. Draw a line between the linked consonants and vowels.

1. What is your account number?
2. Thank you for calling.
3. It's been out all day.
4. Our crews are doing their best.

**C** Read the sentences in 2A and 2B with a partner.

## 3 Use *so…that*, *such…that*, and *such a/an…that*

**A** Study the chart. Complete the sentences below with *so*, *such*, or *such a/an*.

| So…that, such…that, such a/an…that | |
|---|---|
| The prices were so high<br>They had such high prices | that she decided to look at some other companies. |
| It was such an expensive plan | |

**GRAMMAR NOTE**

- Use *so*, *such*, *such a/an* + *that* to show a result.
- Use *so* with an adverb or an adjective.
- Use *such* or *such a/an* with an adjective + a count noun(s).

1. The service was __so__ slow that I changed plans.
2. That phone was _____ popular item that it's sold out.
3. This is _____ busy store that it's crowded even at 9:00 a.m.
4. They have _____ expensive contracts for phone service!

**B** Work with your classmates. Discuss the question.

What kind of news is so important that everyone should pay attention to it?

## 4 Building conversation skills

**A** Look at the picture and the phone conservation in 4B. What is the purpose of the call? How do you know?

**B** Listen to the sample conversation. Why does the clerk apologize?

2-41

**A:** Thank you for calling Leemart's. How can I help you?

**B:** Hi. I'm interested in the microwave oven you have on sale. It's model TC0208.

**A:** The TC0208? I'm sorry; that one is sold out.

**B:** They're sold out?

**A:** Yes, I'm afraid so.

**B:** What about model AJ0629? It's on sale too, right?

**A:** I'm afraid not. That sale ended last week. We do have others on sale, though.

**B:** Oh, that's disappointing. I'll have to think about it. Thanks anyway.

**IN OTHER WORDS…**

Apologizing
*I'm sorry, (but)…*
*Yes, I'm afraid so.*
*No, I'm afraid not.*
*Unfortunately…*

**C** Role-play the situation below.

| Talk about | Roles | Instructions | Remember |
|---|---|---|---|
| Helping a customer on the phone | employee | Apologize when you do not have what the customer wants. | Use key phrases from 4B<br>Apologize |
| | customer | Ask about products you are interested in. | |

# 5 Focus on listening for details

**A** Do you agree or disagree with the statement below? Why or why not? Discuss your opinion with a partner and state your reasons.

*Most businesses make it easy to return an item you have bought if there is a problem with the item.*

**B** Prepare to listen. Read the sentences. Predict what you will hear in the conversation.

1. Bill ordered the watch after he saw it ( in a catalog / online ).

2. He's unhappy because the watch is ( dented / scratched ).

3. Bill got his order ( about a week ago / about three weeks ago ).

4. Bill wants to ( return / exchange ) the watch.

5. Bill needs to write the ( item number / RA number ) on the return slip.

6. The number Karen gives Bill is ( 14-603-4 / 40-603-4 ).

 **C** Listen. Circle the correct words in 5B. Compare your answers with a partner.
2-42

# 6 Discuss

**A** Work with a group. How can customer service representatives use people skills and appropriate language to handle customers' questions and complaints? Collaborate to make a chart.

| customer | skill | to say |
|---|---|---|
| Somewhat disappointed | Apologizing | *I'm so sorry.* |
| Extremely angry | | |

**SPEAKING NOTE**

**Keeping a conversation on topic**
*To get back to our topic…*
*That's very interesting. Now to get back to what we were talking about…*
*Let's put that on hold for a minute until we decide…*
*Let's make a note of that idea and look at it after we…*

A: *I think you can use empathy when a customer is disappointed. I remember one time when I…*

B: *That's very interesting. Now to get back to what we were talking about…*

**B** Report the results of your discussion to the class.

*We think that customer service representatives need to be…*

---

## ▶▶ TEST YOURSELF

Assess your participation in the group and class discussions. Today I was able to…

☐ listen effectively    ☐ report a problem

☐ speak accurately    ☐ ask questions

## 1 Read

**A Talk about the question with your classmates.**

1. What does consumer protection mean to you?

2. Can you give examples of a company recalling products because they were unsafe?

**B Read the definitions.**

issue: (v) to send out

policy: (n) a rule

potentially: (adv) possibly

rating: (n) how good something is

**C Preview the reading. Look at the title of the article. What can you guess that the article will be about? Circle the answer.**

a. Organizations that protect consumers

b. Organizations that consumers protect

**D Read the article. Which government agencies protect consumers?**

> **READER'S NOTE**
>
> Writers sometimes use important words or phrases that are new to the reader. Reading the sentences around these new words can help the reader learn the meaning of the new words.

### Who's Watching Out for Consumers?

Have you ever heard the saying "Buyer beware"? Many products today are so complicated that it's difficult to evaluate them before you buy. Luckily, consumers have some help.

The U.S. government has several consumer-protection offices. The Consumer Product Safety Commission (www.cpsc.gov) protects the public from potentially dangerous consumer products. CPSC's work to ensure the safety of products like toys, power tools, and household chemicals has led to a decline in the rate of deaths and injuries caused by consumer products since its creation by Congress in 1972.

When a product is unsafe, the CPSC may issue a recall. Consumers who have bought the product can return it either to be fixed or to get their money back.

The Federal Trade Commission (www.ftc.gov) also protects consumers. The FTC monitors[1] advertising to be sure that it is truthful. The FTC also regulates[2]

product warranties and the information you see on product labels.

Some industries have their own consumer-protection policies. The video game and movie industries, put ratings on their products so that parents can decide which movies or games are okay for their children.

Private organizations protect consumers, too. Organizations like Consumer Reports (www.consumerrerpots.org) test and compare hundreds of products and then report the results to their members. These reports help consumers decide which shampoo, insurance plan, or car to buy. So remember that you can get help before you buy a product and protection after you buy it.

[1]monitor: to check or watch something
[2]regulate: to control or supervise through rules or laws

Source: *Consumer Product Safety Commission (CPSC)*

**E** Read the article again. What is the writer's main purpose? Underline the information that supports your answer.

**F** Work with a partner. Ask and answer the questions.

1. What kinds of products does the CPSC work with?
2. What is a *product recall*?
3. What kinds of work is the FTC responsible for?
4. What do the video game and movie industries do to help parents?
5. Where can you find ratings on products like cars and insurance policies?

# 2 Word study

**A** Study the chart. Complete the sentences below.

| The suffix *-ful* |
| --- |

The suffix *-ful* means *full of*. Add *-ful* to the end of some nouns to form adjectives. Add *-fully* to form adverbs.

Notes: The suffix *-ful* has only one *l*. Sometimes there is a spelling change: *beauty—beautiful care—careful—carefully*

The box said "Handle with **care**", so I was **careful** when I opened it.
Then I read the instructions **carefully**.

| noun | adjective | adverb | | noun | adjective | adverb |
| --- | --- | --- | --- | --- | --- | --- |
| beauty | beautiful | beautifully | | pain | painful | painfully |
| care | careful | carefully | | truth | truthful | truthfully |
| help | helpful | helpfully | | hope | hopeful | hopefully |
| use | useful | | | | | |

1. This tool isn't very _useful_ . I'm disappointed in it.
2. Do you think this ad is _____ ? It seems pretty hard to believe.
3. The FTC's website is easy to use. It was really _____ when I wanted to file a complaint.
4. I filled out the complaint form _____ . I described exactly what happened.
5. I burned my hand on my new stove. The burn was very _____ .
6. I'm _____ that I'll get a good price when I sell my car.

**B** Write a sentence about each topic. Use the underlined word in your sentence.

1. something you have read that wasn't <u>truthful</u>

_____

2. something you always do <u>carefully</u>

_____

3. an extremely <u>useful</u> product you have bought recently

_____

## 3 Talk it over

**A** Look at the pie chart and read the note. Complete the sentences and answer the questions.

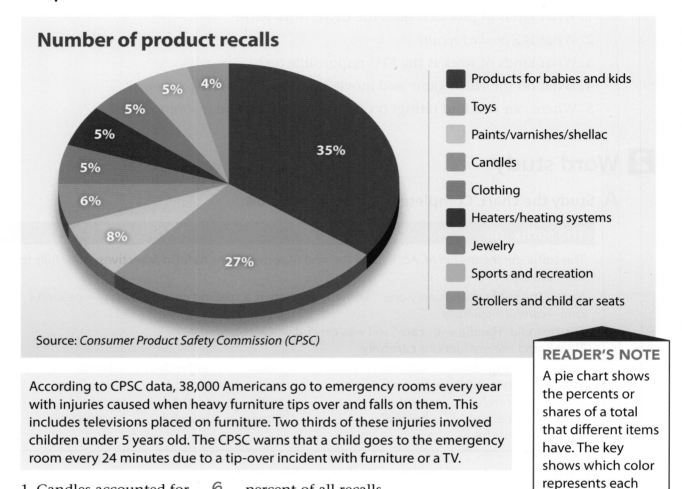

**Number of product recalls**

- Products for babies and kids — 35%
- Toys — 27%
- Paints/varnishes/shellac — 8%
- Candles — 6%
- Clothing — 5%
- Heaters/heating systems — 5%
- Jewelry — 5%
- Sports and recreation — 5%
- Strollers and child car seats — 4%

Source: *Consumer Product Safety Commission (CPSC)*

> **READER'S NOTE**
> A pie chart shows the percents or shares of a total that different items have. The key shows which color represents each item in the pie.

According to CPSC data, 38,000 Americans go to emergency rooms every year with injuries caused when heavy furniture tips over and falls on them. This includes televisions placed on furniture. Two thirds of these injuries involved children under 5 years old. The CPSC warns that a child goes to the emergency room every 24 minutes due to a tip-over incident with furniture or a TV.

1. Candles accounted for ___6___ percent of all recalls.
2. Over half of recalls were for items used by and for _____ .
3. About one quarter of all recalls were for _____ .
4. Clothing and jewelry together account for about _____ percent of product recalls.
5. About _____ visits to emergency rooms every year involve furniture or a TV falling on a child under the age of 5.

**B** Work with a partner to discuss the questions.

1. Are you surprised by any of the data on recalls? Why or why not?
2. Why do you think so many recalls involve products for children?
3. How can people prevent furniture and TVs from tipping over?
4. How can the government make people aware of the danger of furniture tipping over?

---

## ⏻ BRING IT TO LIFE

Visit several stores or shopping websites. Make notes about their return and exchange policies. Bring your notes to class and compare them in a group.

**A** Listen to the staff meeting. What are they discussing?

2-43

**B** Listen to the staff meeting again. Then put a check next to each suggestion that is mentioned.

2-43

_____ hire more new people                  _____ know the store well

_____ say "I don't know"                     _____ listen actively

_____ summarize the customer's problem       _____ take turns

**C** Listen again. What is the reason the supervisor is having this staff meeting? Tell a partner what you heard.

2-43

**D** Read the chart. Discuss the questions below with your class.

| When you want to help teammates participate, you can | |
|---|---|
| **Do this** | **Say this** |
| • Look at your teammate | What do you think _____ ? |
| • Hold your hand out (palm up) toward your teammate | It's your turn. |
| | Tell us your ideas. |
| • Tilt your head towards your teammate | You're up next!* |
| | Let's give _____ a turn. |

*less formal

1. Why is it important for people to participate in a group discussion?

2. What else can you do with your hands to encourage a teammate to participate?

**E** Work with a partner. Read the problems and make suggestions.

> **Opportunity**
>
> A customer looks lost.
>
> A customer asked two employees where an item is and got two wrong answers.
>
> A customer thinks an item is defective, but it isn't.
>
> A customer has been waiting in line for half an hour and is getting upset.

**F** Have a staff meeting.

1. Work with a group to make a list of three more possible customer problems.

2. Choose one person to run the staff meeting. Everyone else take turns bringing up customer problems and suggesting solutions.

A: _We need to talk about customer service problems. What are some things you can do if...?_

B: _I always try..._

A: _That sounds good. Isa, you're up next!_

# TEAMWORK & LANGUAGE REVIEW

**A** **Look at the picture. Collaborate to select the correct words. Explain your choices.**

1. The line is ( so / such a ) long! And it's only 8 a.m. I'm very ( surprising / surprised ).

2. I would be ( very / not at all ) ( bored / boring ) without all these ( interested / interesting ) customers.

3. I am ( pretty / a little ) ( disappointed / disappointing ) with this blouse. It's ( such / so ) poorly made!

4. Your reason for returning the sweater is ( confused / confusing ) to me.

5. I bought this sweater online. And I'm ( pretty / extremely ) unhappy. It is ( stain / stained ).

6. I am so relieved! That experience was ( a little / really ) ( confused / confusing ).

7. This is terrible! I have ( such a / very ) tight schedule and the line is moving ( somewhat / extremely ) slowly!

**B** **Take turns identifying the speaker for each statement in A. Explain your choice.**

*I think Sally says #6. She's so relieved because she's finished.*

**C** **Complete the sentences with *so*, *such*, or *such a/an*. Discuss your answers with your team.**

1. Apparel 44 is a good company. We have ___such___ great products that being a customer service representative here is easy.

2. We have _____ excellent guarantee that customers can feel good about shopping with us.

3. Our sales are _____ popular that we usually work extra hours during a sale.

4. Our training was _____ good that I'm almost always able to help customers even when they are upset.

5. We have _____ large number of products that it took me a while to learn about all of them.

**D** **Work in a team. Follow the steps below to complete the task.**

1. Assign team roles: manager, director, editor, actors.

2. Choose a problem from the list or a different problem.

3. Write a conversation between a customer and a customer service representative about the problem and a solution.

4. Rehearse your conversation. Act it out for the class.

**Problems**
- something you bought is defective
- a gift you were given is the wrong size and you want to exchange it
- your phone or internet service is not working
- something you ordered online has not arrived

**E** **Interview three classmates. Write their answers.**

1. What is the best shopping experience you have had? What is the worst?

2. What shopping advice would you give someone who has just moved to your area? Why?

3. Would you rather buy shoes at a thrift store, at a department store, or online? Why?

**F** **Report your results for Exercise E, #2 to the class. Make a graph with your class results.**

## PROBLEM SOLVING

2-44

**A** **Listen and read about Lidia.**

> Last week, Lidia's neighbors had a yard sale. Lidia doesn't know her neighbors very well, but she went to the yard sale and bought a vacuum cleaner for $25. When she got it home, however, she noticed some problems with it. It made a lot of noise, and it didn't really clean very well. Lidia knows that there are no guarantees at yard sales, but she is unhappy that her neighbors didn't tell her about the problems.

**B** **Work with your classmates. Respond to the prompts.**

1. Identify Lidia's problem.

2. Make a list of possible solutions for Lidia. For each solution, discuss the possible consequences.

UNIT

9 Take Care!

A LOOK AT
■ Health and wellness
■ Forms of advice
■ Team skills

## LESSON 1 VOCABULARY

## 1 Identify health history vocabulary

**A** Collaborate with your classmates. Brainstorm things people do to stay healthy and live a long life.

**B** Read the article. How many secrets for a long life does Althea give?

### Riverside NEWS

Riverside resident Althea Jones turned 101 years old yesterday! Her friend Beatriz Garza interviewed her about her secrets for a long and healthy life.

"Heredity is one of the reasons for my long life," Ms. Jones said. "My great-grandmother was 94 years old when I was born. Most of the women in my family have had long lives. I'm grateful for that kind of heredity."

Ms. Jones says taking care of your health is important too. "Checkups!" she says. "I've seen the doctor and the dentist for checkups every year."

Ms. Jones believes in early detection of health problems. "You have to look for small health problems early so they don't become big problems later on. I have the medical tests my doctor recommends."

If you know Ms. Jones, you know she stays active. She played tennis until she was in her 80s, and she still loves to swim and you'll see her outside taking a walk almost every day. She's a role model for an active lifestyle!

Ms. Jones has one more tip: good nutrition. "I don't eat a lot of meat, and I have fresh vegetables every day. Like they say, you are what you eat!"

**C** Work with a partner. Match the words with the definitions.

_d_ 1. active lifestyle
___ 2. dental checkups
___ 3. early detection
___ 4. good nutrition
___ 5. heredity
___ 6. medical screenings
___ 7. yearly physicals

a. regular visits to the dentist
b. tests to look for health problems
c. checkup with a doctor every year
d. doing things and not sitting around
e. characteristics you get from your family
f. looking for problems before they become big
g. eating healthy foods

 **D** Listen to the interview. Check your work in 1C

3-02

## 2 Learn vocabulary for medical conditions

**A** Look at the medical history form. Circle five problems Althea Jones has had.

### MEDICAL HISTORY FORM

**Name:** Althea Jones                           **Physician:** Dr. Suveena Herat

| | YES | NO | | YES | NO |
|---|:---:|:---:|---|:---:|:---:|
| Childhood diseases | ☑ | ☐ | Chronic cough (cough that does not get better) | ☐ | ☑ |
|   Measles | ☑ | ☐ | High blood pressure | ☐ | ☑ |
|   Mumps | ☐ | ☑ | Heart disease | ☐ | ☑ |
|   Chicken pox | ☑ | ☐ | Weakness in arms or legs | ☑ | ☐ |
| Recent weight gain or loss | ☐ | ☑ | Chest pain or other symptoms of heart disease | ☐ | ☑ |
| Frequent or severe headaches | ☐ | ☑ | | | |
| Diabetes | ☐ | ☑ | Family history of heart disease (Explain below) | ☑ | ☐ |
| Allergies to medications | ☑ | ☐ | | | |
| If yes, which medications? | | | *My mother and grandmother had heart disease.* | ☑ | ☐ |
| *I'm allergic to penicillin.* | ☑ | ☐ | | | |

**B** Work with a partner. Complete the doctor's notes with the words in 2A.

Ms. Jones is very healthy. She maintains an active lifestyle and has had regular medical screenings. There is a family history of heart _____. However, Ms. Jones has no _____ of heart disease. She has
           1                     2
some _____ in one leg. She sometimes has headaches, but they are mild, not _____. She has an
        3                      4
occasional, but not _____, cough. It is controlled with over-the-counter medication. She is _____
        5                      6
to penicillin.

**C** Conduct research. Record your team's responses to the questions below. Report the results.

1. Which is more important to a person's health—heredity or lifestyle? Why?
2. What are the advantages of checkups and medical screenings?
3. What are the three most important things people should do to protect their health?

**D** Report the results of your research.

*Our team agrees that _____ but we disagree about _____ . Some team members think _____ , but others _____ .*

## ▶ TEST YOURSELF

Work with a partner. Take turns reading and listening to the definitions in 1C.

**Partner A:** Read definitions 1–4. Partner B: Listen and write the vocabulary words.
**Partner B:** Read definitions 5–7. Partner A: Listen and write the vocabulary words.

# **1** Prepare to write

**A** **Look at the picture and skim the blog post. Talk about the questions with your class.**

1. Is this a formal or informal style of writing? How do you know?

2. What does the writer want her readers to do?

**B** **Listen and read the blog post.**

3-03

## Adventure Days

Photos (51

**June 29**

Hi, friends,

Thank you for your nice notes after my post about visiting Ellis Island. If you haven't been there, I really encourage you to go! It's fascinating.

I haven't blogged in a few weeks, so it's time to catch up. I got a surprise at my last physical—my doctor said my blood sugar is too high and I'm at risk of becoming pre-diabetic! That means if I don't watch my weight and how I eat, I could develop diabetes (a disease that causes a person's body to have trouble controlling the amount of sugar in the blood). That was a wake-up call!

 I took her advice, and decided to cut back on* processed foods (that's convenience foods and foods with chemicals added) and sugar. I have a real sweet tooth, and I was eating too many sweet snacks. I decided to cut out* sugar on weekdays. And it's working! I've already lost a couple of pounds.

So here's what I want to say to all of you: good health is important! If you haven't had a checkup lately, go get one. What you don't know CAN hurt you. Get out there and be active. And if you need to change your diet, do it. It won't be easy at first. I thought, "Oh, just a little ice cream won't hurt," but after a few weeks, I didn't want sweet snacks all the time.

So that's my advice for today. If I can do it, you can. Good health is the best preparation for the next adventure!

Marisol
Leave a Reply

> **WRITER'S NOTE**
> Use parentheses or explanations with *that is* or *that means* to define words or when you are using them in a special way.

\* *cut back on* = use less of
*cut out* = stop using completely

**C** **Study the blog post. Answer the questions.**

1. Why is Marisol writing this post?

_____

2. What three things does Marisol want to persuade her readers to do?

_____

3. Is Marisol effective in convincing you to take her advice? Why or why not?

_____

## 2 Plan and write

**A** **Talk about the questions with your class. Take notes.**

1. Which lifestyle changes are easy to make? Which changes are difficult?

2. What are two ways to break a bad habit or to start a good habit?

**B** **Write a blog post to persuade your readers to take your advice on a health issue. Use the model blog post in 1B and your answers to the questions in 2A.**

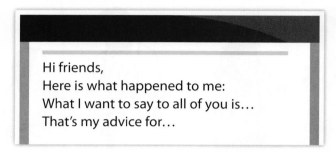

Hi friends,
Here is what happened to me:
What I want to say to all of you is…
That's my advice for…

## 3 Get feedback and revise

**A** **Use the editing checklist to review your writing. Check (✓) the true sentences.**

☐ I talked about a lifestyle change I want to persuade people to make.

☐ I used parentheses or *that is/that means* to define ideas or words.

☐ I wrote about how making a change helped me.

☐ I indented each paragraph.

**B** **Exchange emails with a partner. Read and comment on your partner's work.**

1. Point out an idea that you think is persuasive.

   *Your sentence, "So here's what I want to say…" is very convincing.*

2. Give feedback about the post. Check your understanding.

   *I'm not sure I understand this sentence.*

   *I think you need to be more _____ here.*

**C** **Use the checklist and your partner's feedback to revise your writing.**

---

## ▶▶ TEST YOURSELF

Complete the following sentences. Share your responses with your teacher.

1. After this writing lesson, I can…
2. I need more help with…

# 1 Use different forms of advice

**A** Read the advice. Answer the questions below.

> You should eat more healthy food. You ought to exercise more.

> You shouldn't stay up so late. You'd better drink less coffee.

> You had better not go to school today.

1. What should the man cut back on? What should he start doing?

2. What does the woman do that she shouldn't do?

3. Do we know if the girl will go to school tomorrow?

**B** Study the charts. Circle the sentence in 1A that gives the strongest advice.

| Advice with *should*, *had better*, and *ought to* | | | | | |
|------|------|------|------|------|------|
| You | **should** **ought to** | eat less junk food. exercise more. | You | **shouldn't** | stay up so late. |
| You | **had better** | drink less coffee. | You | **had better not** | go to school today. |

**GRAMMAR NOTE**

Use *had better* to give strong advice or to tell someone to do something.
In informal conversations, people often say "You better" instead of "You'd better."

**C** Look at your answers in 1A and 1B. Complete the statements below.

**Language connection:** Forms of advice

Use *should* and *ought to* to _____. Their meaning is
                                (give advice/agree with someone)
_____ . In the U.S., people don't usually use _____ in negative
(the same/different)                                        (should/ought to)
statements. *Had better* is used to give _____ advice. *He'd better* is a short
                                         (stronger/less strong)
form of _____ .
        (he had better/he would better)

**D** Work with a partner. Match the sentences.

  _c_  1. You look very tired today.

  _____ 2. She eats a lot of sugar.

  _____ 3. Our diet isn't very healthy.

  _____ 4. We need to lose weight.

  _____ 5. She has a lot of headaches.

a. She shouldn't eat so many cookies.

b. We ought to exercise every day.

c. You should get more sleep.

d. She'd better see a doctor.

e. We should eat more green vegetables.

**E** Work in a team. Edit the sentences. Write the corrected sentence.

1. You should to be careful when you lift heavy boxes. _____

2. You ought stay home from work if you can. _____

3. You did better go to the clinic to see the nurse. _____

# 2 Learn the difference between forms of advice

**A** Study the chart. Write two more examples of the strongest types of advice.

| Advice and strong advice | | | GRAMMAR NOTE |
|---|---|---|---|
| mild | should, ought to | You should get some rest. | *Have got to* is as strong |
| strong | had better | You'd better go to the clinic. | as *have to* and *must*, but is |
| stronger | must, have to, have got to | You have to take this medicine. | less formal. |

1. _____

2. _____

**B** Categorize the advice. Write *M* for mild, *S* for strong, or *SR* for stronger.

  _SR_ 1. You've got to see a doctor.

  _____ 2. You'd better see a doctor.

  _____ 3. You must see a doctor.

  _____ 4. You should see a doctor.

**C** Write your own advice. Use the advice words from the chart in 2A in each sentence.

| should | ~~ought to~~ | had better | have to |
|---|---|---|---|

1. A classmate says, "I'm sick. I have a fever."

    You say, "_You ought to go home._ ."

2. A co-worker says, "I just cut my hand. It's bleeding."

    You say, "_____ ."

3. Your teacher says, "I have a cold."

    You say, "_____ ."

4. Your friend says, "I hurt my finger. I can't move it."

    You say, "_____ ."

## 3 Listen for different forms of advice to determine the strength

Listen to two speakers give advice. Who gives stronger advice? Check (✓) *Speaker A* or *Speaker B*.

|     | Speaker A | Speaker B |
| --- | --------- | --------- |
| 1.  | ✓         |           |
| 2.  |           |           |
| 3.  |           |           |
| 4.  |           |           |
| 5.  |           |           |
| 6.  |           |           |

## 4 Use *should, had better, have to,* and *must* to talk about your opinions

**A** **Think about your answers to the questions.**

1. What are things people should do when they have a cold?

2. What is one thing people ought to do for their health? What is one thing they should not do?

3. Imagine that a friend at work begins to feel really sick. What had she better do?

**B** **Work with a partner. Write two more questions.**

1. _____

2. _____

**C** **Work in a team. Ask and answer the questions in 4A and 4B. Take notes on your teammates' answers.**

Matt: *What do you think people should do when they have colds?*

Lois: *I think they should drink tea. What about you, Pedro?*

Pedro: *I think…*

---

## ▶▶ TEST YOURSELF

Close your book. Refer to your notes and write five sentences using the information you learned about your classmates. Use *should, had better, have to,* and *must.*

Lois thinks that people ought to drink tea when they have a cold, but Pedro thinks …

## **1** Learn ways to ask and answer questions at a medical visit

🔊 3-05 **A** Listen to the conversation. Why is Sora at the health-care center today?

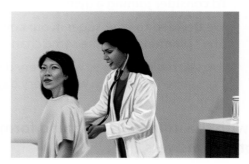

🔊 3-05 **B** Listen again for the answers. Compare answers with your partner.

1. What are Sora's health concerns?

2. What is Sora already doing for her health?

3. What else does the health-care worker recommend?

🔊 3-06 **C** Listen. Write the words Sora uses to confirm the health-care worker's advice.

1. _____ eat well and get more exercise?

2. _____ try to relax, and cut back on salt?

3. _____ schedule a checkup for a year from now?

## **2** Practice your pronunciation

🔊 3-07 **A** Listen to the pronunciation of *s* and *ch* in these words. How are they different?

| Pronunciation of *s* | | Pronunciation of *ch* | |
|---|---|---|---|
| since | sugar | checkup | headache |

🔊 3-08 **B** Circle the sound of the underlined letters in these words. Then listen and check.

1. in<u>s</u>urance ( s / sh )     3. stoma<u>ch</u> ( ch / k )     5. <u>ch</u>ange ( ch / k )

2. <u>s</u>erving ( s / sh )     4. ea<u>ch</u> ( ch / k )     6. <u>ch</u>ronic ( ch / k )

🔊 3-09 **C** Say the sentences with a partner. Then listen and check your pronunciation.

1. She should not serve sugar.     3. I have to change my health insurance.

2. She has a stomachache.     4. I shouldn't eat it. I'm sure it's sweet.

Talk about changes to diet and exercise    **139**

## 3 Use verbs with gerunds and infinitives

**A** Study the chart. Underline 3 examples of an infinitive. Circle 3 examples of a gerund.

| Verbs with gerunds and infinitives | | | |
|---|---|---|---|
| Verb + gerund | quit<br>consider | avoid<br>feel like | He **quit smoking** ten years ago.<br>I'd **consider joining** a gym. |
| Verb + infinitive | decide<br>plan | agree<br>need | We **decided to limit** sugar in our coffee.<br>She's **planning to make** some changes. |
| Verb + gerund<br>or infinitive | start<br>like | continue<br>prefer | I've **started walking** to work every day.<br>I've **started to walk** to work every day. |

**B** Work with a partner. Complete the sentences with the infinitive or gerund form of the verbs in parentheses. Some items have two correct answers.

1. What do you do when you don't feel like ___exercising___ ? (exercise)

2. Which types of exercise do you like _____ ? (do)

3. What did you decide _____ in your diet? (change)

4. I'm going to start _____ more whole, unprocessed foods. (eat)

5. Take my advice. You have to quit _____ . (smoke)

## 4 Building conversation skills

**A** Look at the picture and the conversation in 4B. What is the purpose of the conversation? How do you know?

**B** Listen to the sample conversation. What does Tony want to prevent?

3-10

**A:** You've lost some weight since your last visit, Tony.

**B:** Well, I'm trying to eat smaller portions. I'm concerned about diabetes.

**A:** Well, reducing the calories you take in is great.

**B:** OK. Is there anything else you'd recommend?

**A:** Try to exercise 30 minutes five days a week.

**B:** So I should watch calories and exercise, right?

**A:** Yes, that's it. And it's great that you're thinking about prevention now.

**IN OTHER WORDS...**

Confirming advice
*So I should…(?)*
*So I need to…, right?*
*So I'm supposed to…(?)*
*So I have to…, is that correct?*

**C** Role-play the situation below.

| Talk about | Roles | Instructions | Remember |
|---|---|---|---|
| A health and wellness checkup | physician's assistant | Your patient has made a positive change. Listen to your patient's concerns and offer advice on what to do, cut back on, or cut out. | Use key phrases from 4B |
| | patient | Talk about a change you've made and why. Ask for other recommendations to help you. Confirm the advice you hear. | Confirm advice |

# 5 Focus on listening for details

**A** Do you agree or disagree with the statement below? Why or why not? Discuss your opinion with a partner and state your reasons.

*Immunizations are not just for children. Adults should make sure they get the shots they need to protect themselves.*

**B** Prepare to listen. Read the sentences. Predict what you will hear in the interview.

1. Mr. Gomez cut himself ( on a machine / in the garden ).
2. The health worker gives Mr. Gomez antibiotic ( ointment / pills ).
3. Mr. Gomez had a tetanus shot ( less than 10 / more than 20 ) years ago.
4. The health worker gives Mr. Gomez ( two shots / one shot ) on this visit.
5. Mr. Gomez ( has to / doesn't have to ) come to the clinic again next week.

**C** Listen. Complete the sentences in 5B. Compare your answers with a partner.

3-11

## Prevent Tetanus!
### Get immunized.

Tetanus is a serious disease. Tetanus germs live in dirt and soil. If you get a cut, check with your health-care provider. Adults need a tetanus booster shot every 10 years.

If you work in a health-care setting, check with your doctor for other immunizations you may need.

# 6 Discuss

**A** Work with a group. Read the question and collaborate to make a chart.
*What kinds of health precautions should workers in different jobs take?*

- nursing home workers
- office workers
- construction workers
- day care workers
- emergency workers

A: *So I understand that you think immunizations are just for kids.*

B: *Well, not exactly. I think…*

**B** Report the results of your discussion to the class.

*We think that people who work in…should…*

**AT WORK**

---

## ▶▶ TEST YOURSELF

Assess your participation in the group and class discussions. Today I was able to…

- ☐ listen effectively
- ☐ confirm information and advice
- ☐ speak accurately
- ☐ ask questions

## 3 Talk it over

**A** Look at the table and read the note. Complete the sentences and answer the questions.

### Choosing a Health Plan

Health plans available to families in Robin County vary. In general, the higher the monthly premium, the lower the annual deductible, however, this is not always the case. It is also important to consider the out-of-pocket maximum; this is the most the family will have to pay for health-care services in one year.

| Cost comparison of health care plans for a family of four in Robin County | Plan A | Plan B | Plan C |
|---|---|---|---|
| Estimated* monthly premium | $385 | $280 | $400 |
| Annual out-of-pocket maximum | $12,000 | $10,000 | $9000 |
| Primary care co-pay | $25 | $20 | $35 |

*estimated*: Predicted; not actual

1. The total cost of premiums for one year with Plan A is $4,620 .
2. If each member of a family of four goes to the doctor twice in one year, the total cost of co-pays for the year with Plan B is _____ .
3. "The higher the premium, the lower the out-of-pocket maximum" is true if you compare Plan _____ to Plan _____ .
4. In Plan C, the annual out-of-pocket maximum for a family of four for a year is _____ .
5. The most a family would have to pay in one year with Plan C is _____ .

**B** Work with a partner to discuss the questions.

1. Who should pay for health insurance—employers, the government, or individuals? Why?
2. What do you think the saying "An ounce of prevention is worth a pound of cure" means? Do you agree with the saying? Why or why not? Give examples.
3. Another saying about health is "Early to bed, early to rise, makes a man healthy, wealthy, and wise." What do you think this saying means? Do you agree with the saying?

**C** Talk about your answers with your classmates.

 BRING IT TO LIFE

Think about your community. Brainstorm ways that your community encourages healthy living. Talk about your ideas with your classmates.

**A** Listen to the employees. What are they discussing?

3-12

**B** Listen to the employees again. Then check each thing employees should do that is mentioned.

3-12

_____ tell a manager if they see a problem      _____ use a computer all day

_____ not sit for too long a time      _____ take computer breaks

_____ keep their hands from moving a lot      _____ read the memo about safety

**C** Listen again. What was the reason for each of the items you checked in B? Tell a partner what you heard.

3-12

**D** Read the chart. Discuss the questions below with your class.

| When you want to help the team or class get quiet, you can | |
| --- | --- |
| **Do this** | **Say this** |
| • Raise one hand, palm down, and move it up and down a few times.<br>• Cover your ears and grimace (change your face in a funny way) | Whoa! We're too loud.<br>I can't hear. It's too loud.<br>Could you speak more softly?<br>It's getting noisy, isn't it? |

1. When is it appropriate to help a group get quiet? When is it not appropriate?

2. What else can you do with your hands when you want to help a group get quiet?

3. What should you not say to help a group get quiet?

**E** Work with a partner. Read workplace issues and offer advice.

| Issue | Advice |
| --- | --- |
| back hurts at the end of the day | avoid sitting still for too long |
| hand and wrist hurt | visit the clinic |
| job involves a lot of repetitive motion | talk to the supervisor about safety |

**F** Have an informal conversation about safety at work.

1. Work with a group to make a list of three more possible issues and suggestions about workplace injuries.

2. Take turns bringing up issues and suggestions. Use the ideas from your list and from this page. Give reason(s) for each suggestion.

A: _My hand and wrist hurt._

B: _I think you should…because…_

# TEAMWORK & LANGUAGE REVIEW

## A Collaborate to choose a modal for each sentence. Explain your choices.

| should | ought to | should not | had better |
|---|---|---|---|
| have got to | must | must not | had better not |

1. If the reading is correct, Leo ___must___ seek medical attention immediately.

2. Based on her pulse, Sue _____ continue to exercise daily.

3. _____ take Leo's blood pressure again to be sure the numbers are accurate.

4. _____ do medical screenings for many people at the health fair.

5. _____ get paid for giving these screenings.

6. According to Kyle, Sue _____ worry about her health.

## B Complete the sentences with the gerund or infinitive form of the verb in parentheses. Take turns reading the sentences. Which ones can take both forms?

1. Jean and Lars decided _to make_ some changes in their lives. (make)

2. They considered _____ a health club, but it was a little expensive. (join)

3. Lars started _____ his bike for exercise. (ride)

4. Jean began _____ yoga classes. (take)

5. They agreed _____ a salad with dinner every night. (have)

6. Lars wants _____ less meat. (eat)

7. Jean says she is going to quit _____ . (smoke)

8. Lars says he is going to start _____ more water and less soda. (drink)

## C  Work in a team. Follow the steps below to complete the task.

1. Assign team roles: manager, director, editor, presenters.
2. Choose a problem from the list, or a different problem.
3. Identify possible suggestions or advice for the problem.
4. Write a conversation between a person with the problem and a friend who offers advice.
5. Rehearse your conversation. Act it out for the class.

### Problems
- a serious health problem runs in your family
- health insurance is expensive
- a possible health danger at your workplace

## D  Interview three classmates. Write their answers.

1. How much should people have to pay for health care? Why?
2. Should people with healthy lifestyles pay less for health care? Why or why not?
3. If you could give everyone advice on how to prevent health problems, at home or at work, what would your advice be? Why?

|  | BRONZE | SILVER | GOLD |
|---|---|---|---|
| Monthly Premium | $ | $$ | $$$ |
| Deductible | $5,000 | $3,000 | $1,500 |
| Co-pay | $35 | $30 | none |
| Out-of-pocket Maximum | $10,000 | $6,000 | $3,000 |

## E  Report your results for Exercise D, #2 to the class. Calculate the percentage of your class with each opinion. Make a pie chart of the results.

# PROBLEM SOLVING

3-13

## A  Listen and read about Ivan.

Ivan is worried about his sister, Katya. He thinks that Katya doesn't pay enough attention to her health. Ivan believes in preventing health problems, and he exercises and eats a healthy diet. Katya doesn't exercise. She eats fast-food for dinner several times a week, and she doesn't have health insurance at her job. Katya is an independent person who doesn't like it when people try to tell her what to do. Ivan wants Katya to be healthy, but he doesn't know how to help.

## B  Work with your classmates. Respond to the prompts.

1. Identify Ivan's problem.
2. Make a list of ideas Ivan could try, and a list of things Ivan should not try. For each idea, discuss the possible consequences.

# 10 Get Involved!

## LESSON 1 VOCABULARY

### 1 Identify community-involvement strategies

**A** Collaborate with your classmates. Brainstorm ways to get involved in your community and reasons to do this.

**B** Work with a partner. Talk about the pictures. What happened in this community?

**C** Number the actions in the correct order. The community...

| | |
|---|---|
| _____ implemented the plan | _____ got approval |
| _____ discussed alternatives | _____ proposed a solution |
| __1__ identified a problem | _____ developed a plan |

**D** Listen for information about community involvement. Take notes. Check your work in 1C.

3-14

## 2 Learn about community services

### A Look at the city directory. Which office gets the most telephone calls? Why?

| Department | Services | Extension |
|---|---|---|
| Administration | mayor, city council, city manager | X5510 |
| Child care Services | low-cost daycare | X5511 |
| Health Services | community clinics | X5512 |
| Legal Services | city law clinic | X5518 |
| Parks & Recreation | sports, art, music programs, community centers | X5520 |
| Public Safety | crime prevention, police, fire safety | X5524 |
| Public Works | street and lighting maintenance, building permits | X5529 |
| Senior Services | senior centers, lunch programs | X5530 |

www.citydirectoryww.org

### B Work with a partner. Complete the sentences. Use the words in 2A.

1. Isabel wants to talk to the city manager. She'll call _Administration_ .

2. A traffic light is broken on Main Street. Let's call _____ .

3. Yusef wants to ask about jobs at a community center. He'll call _____ .

4. Maria needs to find child care for her 3-year old. She'll call _____ .

5. Gary wants to ask about a neighborhood watch program to reduce crime. He'll call _____ .

6. If you need to visit a low-cost health clinic, call _____ .

7. Paco needs to talk to a lawyer. He'll call _____ .

8. I want information on lunch programs for my grandmother. I'll call _____ .

### C Conduct research with a team. Look at websites and community newsletters, and/or survey your classmates in order to report on the questions below.

1. What kind of person makes a good community leader? Explain your ideas.

2. Which community services are the most/the least important to you? Why?

### D Report the results of your research.

*Most of our team members think that … makes a good community leader. The most important community services for our team are … and …. For our team, …is the least important because ….*

---

## ▶▶ TEST YOURSELF

Work with a partner. Take turns reading and giving examples of the prompts in 1C.

**Partner A:** Read prompts 1–3. Partner B: Say the steps the community took.
**Partner B:** Read prompts 4–6. Partner A: Say the steps.

# 1 Prepare to write

## A Look at the email. Talk about the questions with your class.

1. How do people help improve their communities?
2. Have you ever tried to solve a problem in your community, school, or workplace? If so, what was the problem? What did you do?

 **B Listen and read the email.**

3-15

Dear Ms. Butler:

I am writing to ask for your help with a problem in our community. I live in the Melrose neighborhood, near the intersection of Pine and Arroyo streets. I am very concerned about the safety of pedestrians who cross the street at this intersection. The traffic light changes too quickly. I think we need to increase the time that the light on Arroyo stays red for cars.

My primary concern is the safety of the people in our community. Older people who walk with canes or walkers cannot make it across the street in time. Parents with children also have a difficult time. I have timed the light and it changes from green to yellow to red in 13 seconds. If the light stayed red for 5 more seconds, everyone would be able to cross safely.

I would like to invite you to visit our neighborhood to see the problem for yourself. Please contact me by email, or at (972) 555-1409. I look forward to hearing from you.
Sincerely,
Alan Hart

**WRITER'S NOTE**

Focus each paragraph on a clear purpose. In this email:

Paragraph 1 introduces the reason for writing and the problem.

Paragraph 2 explains the situation with more detail.

Paragraph 3 asks the reader to do something.

## C Study the email. Answer the questions.

1. Why do you think Mr. Hart starts by saying that he is writing to ask for help?

2. What two examples show that the problem is serious?

3. What are two things he wants?

# 2 Plan and write

## A Talk about the questions with your class. Take notes.

1. What are some things you would like to improve in your community? Why?

2. Who could you write to about these situations?

## B Write an email to a government official. Use the model email in 1B and your answers to the questions in 2A.

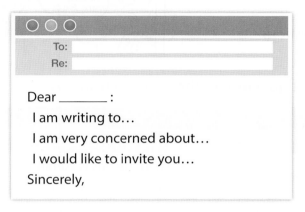

```
To: _____
Re: _____

Dear _____ :
  I am writing to…
  I am very concerned about…
  I would like to invite you…
Sincerely,
```

# 3 Get feedback and revise

## A Use the editing checklist to review your writing. Check (✔) the true sentences.

☐ My email addresses the person I am writing to.

☐ I introduced the problem in the first paragraph.

☐ I explained the problem and gave examples in the second paragraph.

☐ I included my contact information in the third paragraph.

## B Exchange emails with a partner. Read and comment on your partner's work.

1. Point out the sentences that you think are effective.

*Your sentence, "There are…" describes the seriousness of the problem.*

*Your invitation is effective because…*

2. Give feedback about the email. Check your understanding.

*I'm not sure I understand this part of the problem.*

*I think you need to say more about…*

## C Use the checklist and your partner's feedback to revise your writing.

---

## ▶▶ TEST YOURSELF

Complete the following sentences. Share your responses with your teacher.

1. After this writing lesson, I can…

2. I need more help with…

# 1 Use indirect information questions

**A** Read the editorial cartoon. Answer the questions below.

1. Who are the people in the cartoon?

2. What does the woman want to know?

3. Does the man answer the woman's question? Explain your answer.

**B** Study the charts. Underline the indirect question in the cartoon from 1A.

| Indirect information questions | |
|---|---|
| **Direct information question** | **Indirect information question** |
| When **is** the bus **coming**? | Do you know when the bus **is coming**? |
| Where **do** the buses **stop**? | Could you please tell me where the buses **stop**? |
| What **does** the mayor **want**? | Can you tell me what the mayor **wants**? |

**GRAMMAR NOTE**

Indirect questions sound more polite than *Yes/No* or information questions.

**C** Look at the chart in 1B. Complete the statements below.

**Language connection:** Indirect information questions

We can use _____ information questions to make a question more _____ .
(direct/indirect)                                              (polite/useful)

Direct information questions usually begin with a *wh-* question word or _____ . In
(do/how)

indirect information questions the main subject comes _____ the main verb.
(before/after)

**D** Match each situation with an indirect question.

You don't know...

  _b_   1. the location of the bus stop        a. Do you have any idea why the bus is late?

_____ 2. the reason the bus isn't here yet     b. Could you tell me where the bus stop is?

_____ 3. the bus schedule                       c. Do you know which buses stop here?

_____ 4. which buses use this bus stop      d. Can you tell me when the bus will come?

**E** **Work in a team. Edit the sentences. Write the corrected sentence.**

1. Do you know where is the park? — <u>Do you know where the park is?</u>
2. Do you know what does want the teacher? — _____
3. Could you tell me where is the post office? — _____
4. Can you tell me how do you get to city hall? — _____

**F** **Read the answers. Then complete the indirect questions. Practice reading the questions and answers with a partner.**

1. Do you know <u>when the meeting is</u>? (when)
   I think the meeting is at 6 p.m.
2. Do you know _____? (where)
   It's in Room A.
3. Do you have any idea _____? (what)
   I believe the mayor wants to talk about the budget.
4. Could you please tell me _____? (what)
   The mayor's proposal cuts bus service.
5. Can you tell me _____? (which)
   The city cut the parks and senior services budgets.

# 2 Use indirect *yes/no* questions

**A** **Study the chart. Which word means the same as *if* in indirect questions?**

| Direct *Yes/No* questions | Indirect *Yes/No* questions | | |
|---|---|---|---|
| **Is** the bus **coming**? | Can you tell me<br>Could you tell me<br>Do you know | if | the bus **is coming**? |
| | | whether | |
| **Did** they **get** approval? | Can you tell me<br>Could you tell me<br>Do you know | if | they **got** approval? |
| | | whether | |

**B** **Read the direct questions. Then complete the indirect questions.**

1. Is the meeting at 5:00? — Do you know <u>if the meeting is at 5:00</u>?
2. Did they discuss the issue? — Could you tell me _____?
3. Are they going to approve the budget cut? — Do you know _____?
4. Was the mayor at the meeting? — Do you have any idea _____?
5. Did the meeting end on time? — Can you tell me _____?
6. Are they going to meet next month? — Could you tell me _____?

## 3 Listen for indirect questions to determine the meaning

**A** Listen to the conversations. What does each person want to know? Circle the
correct question.

3-16

1. a. When is the next public works committee meeting?

   b. Where is the next public works committee meeting?

2. a. Why is the law clinic closed?

   b. When is the law clinic closed?

3. a. Did they talk about childcare services?

   b. Who do I talk to about childcare services?

4. a. Where is the nearest senior center in your city?

   b. Does your city have any senior centers?

5. a. What does the city manager want?

   b. Where did the city manager go?

6. a. Did the public safety committee discuss my idea?

   b. When did the public safety committee discuss my idea?

**B** Work with a partner. Practice asking indirect questions from the direct questions
in 3A.

*Do you know when the next public works committee meeting is?*

*Do you know where the next public works committee meeting is?*

## 4 Use indirect questions to ask about community services

**A** Write five indirect information or *yes/no* questions about services in your community.

*Do you know what classes the senior center has?*

**B** Work in a team. Ask and answer the questions in 4A. Take notes on your teammates'
answers.

**Kavita:** *Can you tell me what programs the parks and recreation department has?*

**Adam:** *I think they have classes for kids and adults, and a gym.*

---

### ▶▶TEST YOURSELF

Close your book. Write five indirect information questions about schools and colleges in your
area. Exchange questions with a partner and answer the questions.

# 1 Learn ways to comment on an issue in the community

**A** Look at the notice. Listen to the phone calls. How do the callers feel?

3-17

## NOTICE OF PUBLIC HEARINGS

Tomas Noyes, City Clerk, City of Dawson                    **November 15**

**ISSUE:** Plan to build an apartment building next to the 40th Street Park.
**Date: Nov. 20**

**ISSUE:** Proposal to reduce the Summer Jobs for Teens Program from 500 to 150 participants.
**Date: Nov. 28**

**ISSUE:** Proposal to close the Community Police Station in the Hilltop Apartments.
**Date: Dec. 12**

All hearings will take place at 7 p.m. in the Council Chamber, on the 1st floor of the Municipal Building, 440 State St. Interested residents are encouraged to attend and comment on the proposals.

**B** Listen again for the answers. Compare answers with your partner.

3-17

1. What issue is the first caller calling about?

2. What issue is the second caller calling about?

3. How does the city clerk respond to the callers' concerns?

**C** Listen. Write the words the city clerk uses to show that he understands the callers' feelings.

3-18

1. I _____ . You know, there's a meeting about it at 7 p.m. next Tuesday.

2. _____ . If you're interested, there's going to be a public hearing on it.

# 2 Practice your pronunciation

**A** Listen to these long sentences. Notice where the speakers pause.

3-19

1. I'm calling because I heard ^ that the city wants to close the Hilltop Police Station.

2. There's a public hearing on the issue ^ at 7 p.m. tonight, ^ in the Council Chamber.

**B** Listen and mark the pauses (^) in these sentences.

3-20

1. Older people who walk with canes or walkers cannot make it across the street in time.

2. The council members discuss the issue to try to find a solution that works for everyone.

**C** Practice the sentences in 2A and 2B with a partner.

## 3 Use statements with *wh-* and *if/whether* phrases

**A** Study the chart and the picture. What is the man's problem?

### Statements with *wh-* and *if/whether* phrases

| | |
|---|---|
| He doesn't know | where the meeting is. |
| He has no idea | what the meeting is about. |
| He's not sure | when the meeting starts. |
| He can't remember | if the meeting starts at 2 p.m. |
| He forgot | whether the meeting starts at 2 p.m. |

### GRAMMAR NOTE

Use a *wh-* or an *if / whether* phrase after certain expressions to talk about things you don't know for certain.

**B** Work with a partner. Complete the sentences. Circle the correct word or phrase.

**Teddy:** I want to go to the team meeting, but I don't know when ( does it start / it starts ).

**Zoe:** It's at 2:00, but I have no idea what ( is it / it's ) about.

**Teddy:** It's about schedules. I'm not sure what ( the issues are / are the issues ).

**Zoe:** Maybe overtime. I can't remember if ( they sent / did they send ) an email about it.

## 4 Building conversation skills

**A** Look at the picture and the phone conversation in 4B. What is the purpose of the call? How do you know?

 **B** Listen and read the conversation. How does the clerk show understanding of the caller's concern?

3-21

**A:** City clerk's office. Can I help you?

**B:** Hi. This is Maria Delgado. I heard that the city wants to close the Hilltop Community Police Station.

**A:** Yes, that's true.

**B:** But why? It's important for the community, and for the community's relationship with the police.

**A:** I can certainly understand. There's a public hearing on the issue at 7 p.m. on December 12th, in the Council Chamber. I'd encourage you to attend.

### IN OTHER WORDS...

Showing understanding
*I know what you mean.*
*I hear what you're saying.*
*I understand.*
*I can certainly understand.*

**C** Role-play the situation below.

| Talk about | Roles | Situation | Remember |
|---|---|---|---|
| Concern about losing a city service | resident | You heard that the city is planning to close the Troy Street Library. You think the library is important. | Use key phrases from 4B |
| | city clerk | You understand his or her concern. There is a meeting about the issue tomorrow. | Show understanding |

# 5 Focus on listening for details

**A  Talk about the questions with your class.**

1. Why do people attend community meetings and public hearings?

2. How can people get information about meetings and hearings?

3. Is it important for community members to attend these meetings and hearings? Discuss your opinion and state your reasons.

**B  Listen to the recorded message. Circle the correct meeting day, date, time, and location.**

3-22

1. a. Tuesday      b. Thursday             3. a. 7:30 p.m.      b. 7:00 p.m.

2. a. March 23      b. May 23                4. a. Room 210      b. Hearing Room

**C  Listen again. Complete the directions with the words you hear.**

3-22

1. To get to City Hall, take the ___F4___ bus.

2. Go _____ one block to Beech Street to get to the parking lot.

3. Take the elevator to the _____ floor.

4. Follow the signs to the _____ .

5. It will be on your _____ , after Room _____ .

# 6 Discuss

**A  Work with a group. Read and discuss the question for each pair of people. Take notes.**
*Why is it important for _____ to show understanding of _____'s concerns?*

- a clerk and a customer
- an employee and a co-worker
- an employee and a manager

A: *I think it's important for a clerk to show understanding of a customer's concerns because it's a good way to show good customer service.*

B: *I agree. What about an employee and a co-worker?*

A: *An employee and a co-worker? Well, I think…*

> **SPEAKING NOTE**
>
> **Confirm a question before answering**
> A: *What do you think about this question?*
> B: *That question? Well, I guess…*

**B  Report the results of your discussion to the class.**

*We think that it's important for a clerk to show understanding of…because…*

---

## ▶▶ TEST YOURSELF

Assess your participation in the group and class discussions. Today I was able to…

☐ listen effectively      ☐ show understanding of others' concerns

☐ speak accurately      ☐ ask questions

# 2 Word study

## A Study the chart. Complete the chart. Check your spelling in a dictionary. Then complete the sentences below.

### Changing verbs to nouns with -ment

Add -ment to the end of some verbs to form nouns: agree + -ment = agreement

| Verb | Noun | Verb | Noun |
|------|------|------|------|
| agree | agreement | govern | _____ |
| announce | _____ | involve | _____ |
| assign | _____ | state | _____ |

1. Residents have been calling <u>government</u> officials about the dumping problem.
2. The council agreed to a budget increase, and the mayor signed the _____ .
3. They also made an _____ on TV about a new community clean-up program.
4. They want to increase residents' _____ in their communities.

## B Write a sentence about each topic. Use the underlined word in your sentence.

1. an example of community <u>involvement</u> you have seen

_____

2. something you and your classmates are usually in <u>agreement</u> on

_____

3. a <u>statement</u> you would like your local government to make

_____

# 3 Talk it over

## A Think about the questions. Write notes.

1. Whose responsibility is it to keep a community clean? Explain your answer.
2. Why do some people throw litter or trash near roads or in public areas?
3. How can local governments prevent littering and dumping?
4. Should schools teach children about getting involved in their communities? Explain your answer.

## B Talk about your answers with your classmates.

---

 BRING IT TO LIFE

How does your area keep roads and parks clean? Use the library or the Internet to find information on clean-up or Adopt-a-Road programs in your area, or on littering and dumping laws in your area. Bring the information to class and tell your classmates about it.

**A** 🔊 3-23 Listen to the employees. What are they discussing?

**B** 🔊 3-23 Listen to the conversation again. Then put a check next to each idea that is mentioned.

_____ employees helping in the community    _____ volunteering in the evenings

_____ cleaning up trash at a school    _____ helping children with reading

**C** 🔊 3-23 Write the items you did not check in B. Listen again. Correct the items to match ideas you heard in the conversation. Compare your corrections with a partner.

1. _____

2. _____

**D** Read the chart. Discuss the questions below with your class.

| When you want to disagree with someone, you can | |
|---|---|
| **Do this** | **Say this** |
| • Shake your head from side to side. | I disagree. |
| • Squint and tighten your mouth. | I have to disagree. |
| • Tilt your head to one side and squint. | I don't think so. |
| • Take a breath and sigh before speaking. | I don't think that's true. |
| • Roll your eyes.* | Are you kidding?* |
| | No way!* |

\* colloquial, slang, less professional

1. Why does shaking your head show that you disagree?

2. Which of these would you say if you want to disagree with a supervisor? Why?

3. In a formal situation, what should you not do when you disagree with a speaker?

**E** Work with a partner. Read the statements and disagree.

A friend says, "Volunteer work doesn't help a community. People should be paid to do that work."

A supervisor says, "Most employees won't be interested in volunteering."

A co-worker says, "A company volunteer program isn't going to make us feel more like a team."

**F** Have a conversation at work.

1. Work with a group to make a list of five possible workplace volunteer ideas.

2. Choose one person to start the conversation. Take turns bringing up ideas and reasons for and against them. Agree on one idea you will suggest for your workplace.

A: *What kind of program do you think…?*

B: *I think the best idea is…*

C: *I disagree. I think that it would be better…*

# TEAMWORK & LANGUAGE REVIEW

**A** Look at the picture. Collaborate to write indirect questions. Need help? Use the chart.

*Can you tell me what the mall hours are?*
*Do you know where the restroom is?*

| Can you tell me | where... | why... |
|---|---|---|
| Do you know | who... | how... |
| Do you have any idea | when... | how much... |

**B** Write three new indirect questions about the mall using *if*. Ask your teammates your questions. Answer their questions.

1. Do you have any idea if _____ ?

2. Can you tell me if _____ ?

3. Do you know if _____ ?

**C** Read the story. Then complete the sentences. Use the questions in parentheses. Compare answers with your teammates.

1. I don't know ___*who proposed the clean-up.*___
(Who proposed the clean-up?)

2. I'm not sure _____
(How much time did repairs take?)

3. I don't recall _____
(How much did the repairs cost?)

4. I don't remember _____
(Did the donut shop stay open during the clean-up?)

5 We're not sure _____
(Are the shop owners planning another project?)

6. No one knows _____
(Will the mall be renovated this year?)

> Ten years ago, City Mall was in terrible condition. Many shops were closed and there was graffiti everywhere. One shop owner proposed that all the businesses clean up the mall. They contributed money to pay for paint, plants, and benches. Some businesses stayed open during the clean-up, but others were closed. Finally, the repairs were finished. The mall looked beautiful. And it's still beautiful, today.

**D Work in a team. Follow the steps below to complete the task.**

1. Assign team roles: manager, director, editor, actors.
2. Choose a situation from the list, or a different situation.
3. Write a conversation between two neighbors talking about the situation you chose.
4. Rehearse your conversation. Act it out for the class.

**Situations**
- One neightbor wants to volunteer for the city recycling committee, but doesn't know how
- Talk to someone who can do something about broken street lights on the street
- Propose a small new "pocket park" in the neighborhood
- The city should have more activities for senior citizens

**E Interview three classmates. Write their answers.**

1. What should people do if they are unhappy about something in their community?
2. What are the three most important services a community should have for residents?
3. Which community services should be free? Which ones should residents pay for?

**F Report your results for Exercise E, #2 to the class. Make a bar graph with your class results.**

## PROBLEM SOLVING

3-24

**A Listen and read about Teresa.**

Teresa is worried about problems in her neighborhood. There's always a lot of trash in the streets, the sidewalks are cracked, and there's broken glass in the playground. The trees in the area used to be beautiful, but now they're dying because no one takes care of them. People in the neighborhood have stopped taking walks or spending time together outside, and many people don't know their neighbors.

Teresa believes that her neighborhood can solve its problems. She knows that other communities have neighborhood organizations, and she would like to start one in her area. She has a lot of questions, but she's not sure how to get more information.

**B Work with your classmates. Respond to the prompts.**

1. Identify Teresa's problem.
2. Make a list of three or four possible solutions for Teresa.
3. Write four or five polite indirect questions Teresa could ask.

# UNIT 11 Find Us Online!

**A LOOK AT**
- Renting and renters' rights
- Tag questions
- Helping others

## LESSON 1 VOCABULARY

### 1 Identify Internet vocabulary

**A** Collaborate with your classmates. Look at the picture, read the text, and answer the questions.

1. What parts of the web page can you click on?
2. Where can you type or enter information?
3. What is the difference between what you can do with the cursor and the pointer?

**Internet 101**
**M, W 6-9 pm**
**36 hrs**
Learn the basics of searching and using the Internet: navigate the web, **discriminate** between types of sites, **research** topics and keep personal information safe and **secure** from threats.

**B** Use context clues. Mark the words in the class description that help you understand the bold words in the text. Compare your ideas with a partner.

**C** Complete the sentences with the words from the picture. Then listen and check your work. _(3-25)_

1. move the mouse to move the _____ around.
2. click the small *X* to close a _____ .
3. use the _____ to move up and down to choose an item in a _____ .
4. type the _____ of the page you want in the address box at the top.
5. move the mouse to the _____ and then click in the box to change the pointer to a _____ .
6. click on one of the _____ to go to another page on the site.

**D** Listen again. Is the instructor doing a good job? Explain your answer. _(3-25)_

**E** Ask and answer the question with your partner.

In your opinion, what are some of the ways the Internet is most useful?

**164** Identify web resources and tools

## 2 Learn website vocabulary

**A** Look at the website links. Match the links with the definitions.

  b   1. information about the organization that the site belongs to

_____ 2. the website's first page

_____ 3. a list of questions many people have

_____ 4. the organization's phone number, email address, and location

_____ 5. new information recently added to the site

_____ 6. other websites on the same topic

**B** Work with a partner. Practice the conversation. Use the words in 2A.

A: How do I go to the first page of the website?

B: Click on Home.

A: What happens if I click on What's New?

B: You see new information on the website topic.

**C** Conduct research with a team. Survey your classmates and report on the questions below.

1. What are some websites that people in our class like? Why do they like them?

2. Do you have a website? If you do, describe it. If you don't, what would you put on a website if you had one?

**D** Report the results of your research.

*Our team discovered that most of us like...because.....*

*No one has a website, but if we did,...*

## ▶▶ TEST YOURSELF

Work with a partner. Take turns reading and responding to the prompts in 1C.

**Partner A:** Read prompts 1–3. Partner B: Listen and write the vocabulary words.
**Partner B:** Read prompts 4–6. Partner A: Listen and write the vocabulary words.

## 1 Prepare to write

**A** Look at the essay and read the first sentence of each paragraph. Talk about the questions with your class.

1. How would you describe your computer skills? Are you an expert, an experienced user, or a beginner?

2. Has technology changed the way you get information? Give examples.

**B** Listen and read the essay.

3-26

> **WRITER'S NOTE**
> When comparing times, use time expressions to make the times clear for the reader.

### Technology Then and Now
#### by Pedro Sanchez

Ten years ago, I used technology a lot less in my daily life. I used the Internet, but only on a desktop computer at work or at home. I used my cell phone a lot, but just to make calls. When I needed to go online, I waited until I got home. I kept track of things like my family budget or my address book on the computer, but I kept track of other things, like shopping lists, or how much I exercised, on paper. It seems funny now to think about how much I relied on paper back then.

Today, we don't even talk about computers. We talk about devices! I have a smartphone and a tablet computer, and they talk to each other. I can check the wait times at the Department of Motor Vehicles before I go, or the wait time for a bus before I leave the house, and then I can go online or watch a movie while I'm in line. I use an activity tracker to keep track of how much exercise I'm getting, and it really motivates me to stay active. I video chat with my family in El Salvador; it's so much easier now to stay in touch.

Some things haven't changed, though. My family turns all of our devices off during dinner because we want to focus on conversation. I don't use social media much; I'd rather talk to people in person. For birthdays and weddings, I still send a card in the mail. For me, a balance of familiar habits and new ways of doing things works!

**C** Study the essay. Write *T* (true), *F* (false), or *NI* (no information).

___F___ 1. Pedro's use of technology hasn't changed much.

_____ 2. Ten years ago, he used a paper map to get directions.

_____ 3. He has had the Internet at home for more than ten years.

_____ 4. He has taken an online English class.

_____ 5. Pedro sometimes goes online while he's in line.

# 2 Plan and write

**A Talk about the questions with your class. Take notes.**

1. Name some items in your home today that use or connect to a computer.

2. How many of these items did you have ten years ago?

**B Write about changes in your use of technology. Use the model essay in 1B and the questions in 2A and below to help you.**

Paragraph 1: What technology did you use ten years ago? How did you use it?

Paragraph 2: What technology do you use today? How do you use it?

Paragraph 3: What has not changed? What do you still do in the same way?

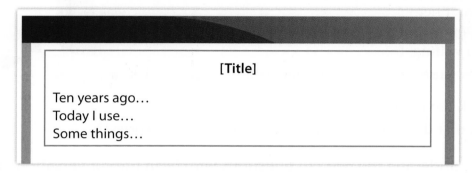

[Title]

Ten years ago…
Today I use…
Some things…

# 3 Get feedback and revise

**A Use the editing checklist to review your writing. Check (✓) the true sentences.**

☐ My first paragraph is about a time in the past.

☐ My second paragraph is about the present.

☐ My third paragraph tells about things that haven't changed.

☐ I used time expressions to make the times clear.

**B Exchange essays with a partner. Read and comment on your partner's work.**

1. Point out a comparison that you think is interesting.

*Your comparison of the way you…ten years ago and now is interesting.*

*Your use of time expressions makes the contrast very clear.*

2. Give feedback about the essay. Check your understanding.

*I'm not sure I understand this sentence.*

*I think you need a _____ here.*

**C Use the checklist and your partner's feedback to revise your writing.**

## ▶▶ TEST YOURSELF

Complete the following sentences. Share your responses with your teacher.

1. After this writing lesson, I can…
2. I need more help with…

## 1 Use tag questions with *be*

**A** Read the conversation. Answer the questions below.

**Abby:** Hi, Leo. You're good with email, aren't you?

**Leo:** Yes, I guess so. Why do you ask?

**Abby:** I'm having trouble emailing my landlord. There was no heat in my apartment this morning.

**Leo:** That's not good. Your landlord is in the building, isn't he?

**Abby:** No, he isn't. I'm going to call him, but I want to put it in writing, too.

**Leo:** That makes sense. I'd be happy to help you.

1. Does Abby think Leo is good with email?

2. Does Leo think that the landlord is in Abby's building? Is Leo correct?

**B** Study the charts. Underline the two tag questions with *be* in the conversation in 1A.

| Tag questions and short answers with *be* | | | |
|---|---|---|---|
| **Affirmative statement** | **Negative tag** | **Agreement** | **Disagreement** |
| You**'re** good with email, | **aren't** you? | Yes, I **am**. | No, I**'m not**. |
| The heat **is off**, | **isn't** it? | Yes, it **is**. | No, it **isn't**. |
| He **was** helpful, | **wasn't** he? | Yes, he **was**. | No, he **wasn't**. |
| **Negative statement** | **Affirmative tag** | **Agreement** | **Disagreement** |
| You**'re not** worried, | **are** you? | No, I**'m not**. | Yes, I **am**. |
| The heat **isn't** working, | **is** it? | No, it **isn't**. | Yes, it **is**. |
| He **wasn't** very helpful, | **was** he? | No, he **wasn't**. | Yes, he **was**. |
| **GRAMMAR NOTES** | | | |

Ask a negative tag question when you think the answer will be *Yes*.
Ask an affirmative tag question when you think the answer will be *No*.

**C** Look at your answers to the questions in 1A. Complete the statements below.

**Language connection:** Using tag questions

Use a negative tag after _____ statement. _____ tags are usually
(an affirmative/a negative)                    (Affirmative/Negative)

contracted. Use a negative tag question when you think the answer will be _____.
(yes/no)

Use _____ tag after a negative statement. Use a _____ before a
(an affirmative/a negative)                              (comma/period)

tag question.

**D  Match the parts of the questions.**

_b_  1. The heaters are old,

_____ 2. This one isn't working very well,

_____ 3. You're not calling the landlord,

_____ 4. The landlord was here,

_____ 5. She's writing an email,

a. isn't she?

b. aren't they?

c. are you?

d. wasn't he?

e. is it?

**E  Complete the sentences with tag questions.**

1. The heater is broken, ___isn't it___ ?

2. The building engineer wasn't in the shop, _____ ? (Two possible answers)

3. You're going to go to work, _____ ?

4. The neighbors were having problems, too, _____ ?

5. It's not too cold today, _____ ?

# 2  Use tag questions with *do* and *did*

**A  Study the chart. Complete the questions below with tag questions.**

| Tag questions and short answers with *do* and *did* | | | |
|---|---|---|---|
| **Affirmative statement** | **Negative tag** | **Agreement** | **Disagreement** |
| You **live** here, | **don't** you? | Yes, I **do**. | No, I **don't**. |
| He **works** on weekends, | **doesn't** he? | Yes, he **does**. | No, he **doesn't**. |
| The heat **worked** Friday, | **didn't** it? | Yes, it **did**. | No, it **didn't**. |
| **Negative statement** | **Affirmative tag** | **Agreement** | **Disagreement** |
| You **don't live** here, | **do** you? | No, I **don't**. | Yes, I **do**. |
| He **doesn't work** on weekends, | **does** he? | No, he **doesn't**. | Yes, he **does**. |
| The heat **didn't work** Friday, | **did** it? | No, it **didn't**. | Yes, it **did**. |

1. The landlord fixed that broken window, _didn't he_ ?

2. You don't want to call him tonight, _____ ?

3. She said we could call her, _____ ?

4. He doesn't work on Mondays, _____ ?

5. He usually fixes things right away, _____ ?

6. They need a helper, _____ ?

**B  Work in a team. Edit the sentences. Write the corrected sentence.**

1. You called me, did you?                        _You called me, didn't you?_

2. Your doorbell doesn't work, doesn't it?     _____

3. The people in 3A just moved in, did they?  _____

4. That looks better, does it?                      _____

5. You don't need anything else, don't you?   _____

## 3 Listen for the verb to determine the tag question

3-27

**Listen to the speakers. Circle the correct tag to complete the question.**

1. a. aren't you?
   b. didn't you?

2. a. don't you?
   b. aren't you?

3. a. do you?
   b. did you?

4. a. is it?
   b. does it?

5. a. is she?
   b. isn't she?

6. a. doesn't it?
   b. do they?

7. a. aren't they?
   b. aren't we?

8. a. did we?
   b. didn't we?

9. a. did it?
   b. didn't it?

## 4 Use tag questions to ask about life experience

**A** Work with a partner. Predict the answers to the questions, but don't check your answers yet.

1. Where is your partner from?
2. Did your partner study English before he or she came here?
3. Does your partner have a job?
4. What does your partner do (what is his or her job)?
5. Is your partner fairly comfortable with technology?

**B** Work with your partner. Ask tag questions to check your predictions in 4A. Answer your partner's questions. Try to add extra information.

A: *You're from Sri Lanka, aren't you?*
B: *Yes, I am. I came here last year.*
A: *You have a job, don't you?*
B: *No, actually, I don't. I…*

> **SPEAKER'S NOTE**
> After a short answer, you can add extra information to help keep a conversation going.

**C** Test your classmates. Ask questions about your partner and answer your classmates' tag questions.

A: *Where's Adil from?*
B: *He's from Thailand, isn't he?*
A: *No, he isn't. He's from Sri Lanka.*

---

## ▶▶ TEST YOURSELF

Close your book. Think of a famous person and five things you think you know about him or her. Write five tag questions about the person. Then test your classmates' knowledge.

*Nelson Mandela was the president of South Africa, wasn't he?*

# 1 Learn ways to offer and respond to help

🔊 **A** Listen to the conversation. What does Abby want to do? What are Leo's
3-28 two suggestions?

🔊 **B** Listen again. Then check (✔) each task that Leo helps
3-28 Abby with. Compare your answers with a partner.

_____ reading an email

_____ signing in to her email

_____ typing in the landlord's address

_____ the length of the message

_____ sending an email

_____ calling the landlord

🔊 **C** Listen. Write the words Leo uses to offer help.
3-29

1. Abby: So I click here in the empty box
and start typing?

   Leo: Yes, but _____ ?

2. Abby: Oh, OK. There we go.

   Leo: _____ ?

# 2 Practice your pronunciation

🔊 **A** Listen to the questions. Notice how the speakers use falling and rising intonation.
3-30

| Falling intonation | Rising intonation |
| --- | --- |
| _The speaker is fairly sure of the answer._ | _The speaker is not sure of the answer._ |
| This is a good website, isn't it? ↘ | This is a good website, isn't it? ↗ |
| You don't use email often, do you? ↘ | You don't use email often, do you? ↗ |

🔊 **B** Listen. How sure are the speakers of their answers? Check _Fairly sure_ or _Not sure_.
3-31

|  | Fairly sure | Not sure |  | Fairly sure | Not sure |
| --- | --- | --- | --- | --- | --- |
| 1. |  |  | 4. |  |  |
| 2. |  |  | 5. |  |  |
| 3. |  |  | 6. |  |  |

**C** Practice the questions in 2A with a partner.

Ask for clarification and offer to help   **171**

## 3 Use question words for clarification

**A Study the chart. Complete the questions below with *what* or *where*.**

| Question words for clarification | |
|---|---|
| **A:** I need help with writing an email. <br> **B:** With what? <br> **A:** With writing an email to the landlord. | **A:** Click in the search box. <br> **B:** Click where? <br> **A:** In the search box, right here. |

1. **A:** The choices are on a pull-down menu.
   **B:** On a _____ ?

2. **A:** Type the address in the URL box.
   **B:** Type the URL _____ ?

**B Work with a partner. Match each sentence with a clarification question. Ask and answer.**

_e_ 1. Click this link first.
____ 2. This link. Then read the FAQ.
____ 3. Twenty. They're by a renters' group from Ohio.
____ 4. Ohio. You can email them with questions.
____ 5. Uh… Why don't you ask Tim to help you?

a. The what?
b. Ask who?
c. From where?
d. With what?
e. Click what?

## 4 Building conversation skills

**A Look at the picture and the conversation in 4B. What is the purpose of the conversation? How do you know?**

**B Listen to the sample conversation. How does Arnie offer to help?**

3-32

**A:** Denise, are you still having trouble with that document?

**B:** Yes, Arnie, I am! I can't make it look right.

**A:** Can I make a suggestion? Why don't you put that part in a table?

**B:** In a what?

**A:** In a table—like a chart, with rows and columns.

**B:** Oh, OK, that's a good idea.

**IN OTHER WORDS…**

Offering help
*Can I make a suggestion?*
*Can I offer a suggestion?*
*Can I suggest something?*

**C Role-play the situation below.**

| Talk about | Roles | Instructions | Remember |
|---|---|---|---|
| Understanding a website | employee | Your co-worker has problems with a website. Offer to help. Suggest using the search box and typing *hours*. | Use key phrases from 4B <br> Offer to help |
| | co-worker | You are having trouble finding a company's hours (when they are open). Ask for clarification. Check if you should click *Go*. | |

AT WORK

# 5 Focus on listening for details

**A** Do you agree or disagree with the statement below? Why or why not? Discuss your opinion with a partner and state your reasons.

*The best way to find a new home is to use the Internet.*

**B** Listen to the interview. Answer the questions.

3-33

1. What are the people talking about?

2. Which person sometimes doesn't speak clearly?

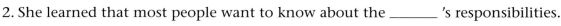

**C** Listen again. Complete the sentences. Compare your answers with a partner.

3-33

1. Malia worked at an apartment rental office when she was in <u>college</u> .

2. She learned that most people want to know about the _____ 's responsibilities.

3. Malia doesn't think it's _____ to learn to design a website.

4. It took Malia about _____ months to design ApartmentSearch.apt.

5. Larry thinks that _____ people use Malia's site.

6. Malia says that _____ of people visit the site every day.

# 6 Discuss

**A** Work with a group. Read the question and collaborate to make a chart. *What kinds of technology skills do employees use at different workplaces?*

- cashiers
- warehouse workers
- delivery drivers
- small business owners
- medical assistants

A: *So we agree that cashiers have to use a cash register...um...*

B: *Good. Let's see what we need to do next. How about delivery drivers?*

> **SPEAKING NOTE**
>
> **Keep a conversation moving**
> I agree. Now what about ...?
> Let's move on to the next one. What do you think about ...?
> Let's see what we need to do next.

**B** Report the results of your discussion to the class.

*We think that most jobs require technology skills. For example, ...*

---

## ▶▶ TEST YOURSELF

Assess your participation in the group and class discussions. Today I was able to...

☐ listen effectively     ☐ offer help

☐ speak accurately     ☐ ask questions

## 3 Talk it over

**A** Look at the messages. How do you think *renthelp101* will answer each question? Underline the words in 1D that support your answer.

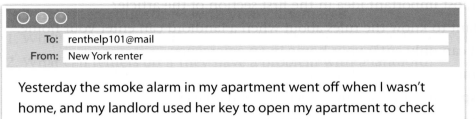

To: renthelp101@mail
From: New York renter

Yesterday the smoke alarm in my apartment went off when I wasn't home, and my landlord used her key to open my apartment to check for fire. Everything was OK; it was just time to change the battery. Should I complain, or did the landlord have the right to come into my apartment?

> **READER'S NOTE**
> The writer's use of informal language helps the reader interpret the tone of a text, and helps to communicate the writer's purpose.

To: renthelp101@mail
From: Miami1016

Hi. I have a question. I am moving out of my rental house, and there is a hole in the wall where I tried to hang up a big picture. Is the landlord entitled to keep some of my security deposit?

Question 1 _____

Question 2 _____

**B** Think about the questions. Write notes.

1. What are some ways landlords and tenants can have a good relationship?
2. How can the Internet help renters and home buyers?
3. What do you think *entitled* means?
4. What do you think *went off* means?

**C** Talk about your answers with your classmates.

---

 BRING IT TO LIFE

Use the Internet or a community resource to find a checklist of things to look at in choosing an apartment or a house. Bring your information to class. Compare checklists with a group. With your group, list the top five things to ask or do when renting a home.

**A** Listen to the conversation. What is the relationship among the people who are talking?

3-34

**B** Listen to the staff meeting again. Then match the words with a definition.

3-34

  _c_   1. sort of                       a. a training class

  _____   2. for starters              b. training website

  _____   3. mandatory             c. in part; not completely

  _____   4. in-person training      d. first

  _____   5. portal                      e. required

**C** Listen again. Who understands each training requirement the best? Who needs help with each requirement? Tell a partner what you heard.

3-34

**D** Read the chart. Discuss the questions below with your class.

| When you want to help someone understand, you can | |
|---|---|
| **Do this** <br> • Point to the item you're talking about. <br> • Spell the word(s) you're talking about. <br> • Repeat the word(s) slowly. <br> • Write the word(s), or draw a picture or diagram. <br> • Use a different word or words. | **Say this** <br> What is unclear?/What isn't clear? <br> What don't you understand? <br> Is this part clear? <br> How can I make it clear? <br> Does this help? <br> Let me explain… <br> Can I help? |

1. Why is *Is this part clear?* better than *What don't you understand?*

2. When is it appropriate to try to help someone who doesn't understand something?

3. Have you ever tried to help someone you didn't know understand something in a public place? What happened?

**E** Have a conversation about requirements at work.

1. Work with a group to make a list of three more kinds of training a workplace might require.

2. Choose one person to be knowledgeable about the training. Everyone else take turns asking questions and bringing up concerns. Make sure everyone understands what they need to do.

A: *Did you see the announcement about…?*

B: *Yes, I did. But I didn't understand…*

C: *What isn't clear?*

# TEAMWORK & LANGUAGE REVIEW

**A** Use tag questions to check your understanding of the story above. Ask and answer the tag questions with your team. Record the questions.

*They're ..., aren't they?    They had ..., didn't they?    There's a ...isn't there?*

**B** Complete the conversation with the tag clarification questions. Explain your choices to your team.

_____ 1.  I found a training class for building maintenance engineers.

_____ 2.  They do routine repairs.

_____ 3.  It covers basic plumbing, carpentry and electrical work.

_____ 4.  The training takes about 10 weeks.

_____ 5.  I'm going to call the college tomorrow.

_____ 6.  They said I should talk to the Dean of career training.

a. How long?
b. When?
c. For who?*
d. Of what?
e. Covers what?
f. Do what?

*It's also possible to say "for whom?"

**C** You are planning your move into a new apartment. Write questions with tags for each situation. Compare questions with your teammates.

1. You think you have to let your current landlord know.

2. You think your current landlords are going to give back your security deposit.

3. You're not sure, but you think the new building doesn't have cable TV.

4. You're fairly certain the rent for the new apartment includes utilities.

5. You don't know for sure, but you think the rent is due on the 15th of the month.

6. You believe that your new landlord speaks both Spanish and Farsi.

7. You are pretty sure that the lease said no parties on weeknights.

8. You can't be sure, but you think the upstairs neighbors are planning to move out.

## D Work in a team. Follow the steps below to complete the task.

1. Assign team roles: manager, editor, actors.

2. Choose a computer problem from the list below, or another problem.

3. Write a conversation between a person who needs help with the problem and a person who knows how to help.

4. Rehearse your conversation. Act it out for the class.

**Computer problems**
- forward an email to a 3rd person
- use a drop-down menu
- get rid of a pop-up ad
- use the scroll bar
- find a web page when you only have the URL

## E Interview three classmates. Write their answers.

1. Are computers and technology important to you? Why or why not?

2. Should public libraries use their budgets to buy books or to provide computers? Why?

3. Some people spend a lot of their time online. Is this a problem? Why or why not?

## F Report your results for Exercise E, #2 to the class. Make a pie chart with your class results.

## PROBLEM SOLVING

3-35

## A Listen and read about Eric.

Eric doesn't know how to use a computer very well. Everyone else in his family is good with computers, and Eric would like to be able to use social media and find information on the Internet.

Eric's brother, Louis, is really knowledgeable about computers and the Internet. Louis has offered to help Eric build his skills, but it's difficult for Eric to learn from his brother. Louis talks quickly, and he likes to show Eric how to do things instead of letting Eric try for himself. Eric finds it really hard to learn that way. Eric likes having his brother's help, but so far, he hasn't learned anything.

## B Work with your classmates. Respond to the prompts.

1. Identify Eric's problem.

2. Brainstorm a list of possible solutions for Eric.

3. Write a conversation between Eric and his brother.

UNIT

# 12 How Am I Doing?

**A LOOK AT**
- Achievements and leadership
- Gerunds
- Responding to feedback

## LESSON **1** VOCABULARY

## **1** Identify achievements

**A** Talk about the questions with a partner.

1. What is something you've done that you're really proud of?

2. What is something you'd like to achieve in your life?

**B** Work with a partner. Talk about the pictures. What are some things Mr. Moya has done in his life?

**C** Number the events in the order they happened to Mr. Moya.

_____ overcome adversity     _____ win a scholarship     _____ achieve a goal

_1_ have a dream     _____ give back to the community     _____ start a business

🔊 **D** Listen for information about Mr. Moya's achievements. Check your work in 1C.
3-36

🔊 **E** Listen again. Complete the sentences about Mr. Moya. Report what you heard.
3-36

1. His dream in high school was _to be elected_ to public office.

2. He was able to _____ because he won a scholarship.

3. He was nervous and excited when he _____ his _____ .

4. He had to overcome adversity when his _____ down.

5. His dream came true when he _____ and became mayor.

6. He wants to _____ because of the support he received.

**F** Work with a team. Create a list of the achievements of the people on your team. Add the words you want to learn to your vocabulary notebook.

# 2 Learn about leadership qualities

**A** Look at the checklist. Check the words that describe you.

DESCRIBE YOUR LEADERSHIP QUALITIES

## ARE YOU A LEADER?

Check (✔) the boxes that describe you.

| IS THIS YOU? | | THEN YOU... |
|---|---|---|
| ☐ | Confident | are usually sure of what you are doing, and that your ideas are good. |
| ☐ | Courageous | don't mind trying something difficult or even a little scary. |
| ☐ | Assertive | aren't afraid to say what you think, but you do it politely. |
| ☐ | Dedicated | believe in what you are doing, and you work hard. |
| ☐ | Practical | are realistic. You know what's possible and what isn't. |
| ☐ | Competent | are good at what you do. |

**B** Work with a partner. Practice the conversation. Use the words in 2A.

A: Which leadership qualities do you think you have?

B: Well, I'm not afraid to say what I think, so I guess I'm pretty assertive. What about you?

A: I'm really dedicated. I believe in what I'm doing.

**C** Conduct research with a team. Survey your classmates in order to report on the questions below.

1. Think about someone you know who has achieved something important. What did the person do before he or she achieved the goal?

2. Talk about someone you know who has good leadership qualities. Which qualities does the person have? How do you know? Report the results of your research.

**D** Report the results of your research.

*Our team talked about... Before he/she..., he/she had to...*

*We think that...has good leadership qualities, like...and...*

*We think so because...*

---

## ▸▸ TEST YOURSELF

Work with a partner. Take turns reading and responding to the prompts in 1E.

**Partner A:** Read prompts 1–3. Partner B: Listen and write the vocabulary words.
**Partner B:** Read prompts 4–6. Partner A: Listen and write the vocabulary words.

# 1 Prepare to write

**A** Look at the scholarship application essay prompt and the essay. Talk about the questions with your class.

1. What are some situations when it's okay to talk about your achievements? What are some situations when it's not okay? Why?

2. Do you like to talk about your plans for the future? Why or why not?

**WRITER'S NOTE**

In a formal essay:

The first paragraph introduces the topic or subject of the essay.

The middle paragraph(s), the body, make the writer's points, with supporting information and details.

**B** Listen and read the essay.

3-37

## Joseph Martin Scholarship Application

Write a short essay (200 words or fewer) in response to these questions: What are your recent achievements? What are your goals for the future? How would this scholarship help you reach your goals?

Name: Victoria Sanchez

I'm really proud of my recent achievements. I am applying for the Martin Scholarship because I believe that a good education is the first step in reaching my goals.

I work hard to achieve the goals I set for myself. When I came to this country, I didn't speak much English, but I studied hard and now I speak English well. In high school, I worked part-time and studied at night, so I was able to help my family and work on my own goals at the same time. I have good evaluations at my job, and last year I received an Outstanding Volunteer award for my work at the City Help Center.

I have several important goals. My first goal is to get a college degree. Then I plan to go to law school. My dream is to be a lawyer. I'd like to be able to help people and contribute to the community that has helped and supported me.

I believe that I have the personal qualities to succeed. Receiving this scholarship would give me the support I need to start my educational journey, and make my dream come true.

**C** Study the essay. Answer the questions.

1. Paragraph 1: What topic(s) is Victoria introducing?

_____

2. Paragraphs 2 and 3: What points does Victoria make? How does she support them?

_____

3. Paragraph 4: What is Victoria's conclusion? Is it convincing?

_____

ACADEMIC

## 2 Plan and write

**A Talk about the questions with your class. Take notes.**

1. What are your recent achievements? What did you do to achieve these things?

2. What are your goals for the future? How will a scholarship help you reach your goals?

**B Write a short essay about your achievements and goals for a scholarship application. Use the model essay in 1B and your answers to the questions in 2A.**

> Write a short essay (200 words or fewer) in response to these questions: What are your recent achievements? What are your goals? How will this scholarship help you reach your goals?
>
> Name: _____
> I'm really proud of my recent achievements…
> I work hard to…
> I have several important goals.
> I believe that…

## 3 Get feedback and revise

**A Use the editing checklist to review your writing. Check (✓) the true sentences.**

☐ My first paragraph introduces the topic.

☐ My middle paragraph(s) make my main points, with supporting information and details.

☐ My final paragraph summarizes the main points and gives my conclusion.

☐ My essay is not more than 200 words.

**B Exchange essays with a partner. Read and comment on your partner's work.**

1. Point out the sentences that you think will help your partner get a scholarship.

   *Your sentence, "I have achieved…" is convincing because…*

   *Your conclusion is very clear.*

2. Give feedback about the essay. Check your understanding.

   *I'm not sure I understand this sentence.*

   *I think you might want to say more about…here.*

**C Use the checklist and your partner's feedback to revise your writing.**

## ▶▶ TEST YOURSELF

Complete the following sentences. Share your responses with your teacher.

1. After this writing lesson, I can…      2. I need more help with…

## **1** Use gerunds after prepositions

**A** **Read the performance review. Answer the questions below.**

| ★★★★★ STAR 5 HOTELS | **PERFORMANCE REVIEW** | |
|---|---|---|
| **Name:** Kim Tran | **Title:** Desk Clerk | **Reviewing Manager:** M. Perez |
| **Period of review:** 7/16 – 6/17 | **Date of review:** 7/10/17 | |
| **Rating Codes:** E= excellent  S= satisfactory  NI= needs improvement | | |
| **Responsibility** | **Rating** | **Comments** |
| Greets hotel guests, answers questions and requests | E | Ms. Tran does a good job of welcoming guests. She cares about helping people. |
| Records information accurately | S | She checks information after recording it. |
| Takes phone messages | NI | She needs to work on taking messages. |

1. What does Ms. Tran do very well?

2. What does she need to do more carefully?

3. Should she work on getting better at managing multiple tasks at the same time? Why or why not?

**B** **Study the chart. Circle the 4 examples of gerunds after prepositions in 1A.**

| **Gerunds after prepositions** |
|---|
| **Preposition + gerund** |
| She does a good job **of welcoming** guests. |
| She knows a lot **about managing** the front desk. |
| Instead **of getting** a promotion, she got a raise. |
| She needs to work **on recording** information accurately. |

**C** **Look at 1A and 1B. Complete the statements below.**

> **Language connection:** Ways to use gerunds with prepositions
>
> Gerunds are the noun form of a verb. Gerunds usually end in _____ .
> (-ed/-ing)
>
> Gerunds are used _____ prepositions like *about, at, for, in, of,* and *to.*
> (after/before)
>
> Gerunds are also used after _____ phrases with prepositions: *She cares about*
> (noun/verb)
>
> _____ *people.*
> (help/helping)

**D Complete the sentences in Kim's review. Use gerunds.**

Kim does a good job of _greeting_ (1. greet) guests and _____ (2. ask) them about their stay when they check out. Before _____ (3. call) me about problems, she tries to solve them herself. Kim is able to solve most routine problems without _____ (4. ask) for help. Instead of _____ (5. sit) down when the desk isn't busy, she helps out by _____ (6. look) for extra work to do. Her work contributes to _____ (7. make) the hotel more welcoming for our guests.

**E Match the parts of the sentences.**

_b_ 1. Kim cares about           a. helping employees.

____ 2. She sometimes worries about     b. doing her job well.

____ 3. The hotel managers believe in     c. remembering people's names.

____ 4. Kim looks forward to         d. learning more about the hotel business.

# 2 Use gerunds after *be* + adjective + preposition

**A Study the chart. What verb is used in all of these sentences?**

| *Be* + adjective + preposition + gerund |
| --- |
| The manager is responsible for evaluating Kim's work. |
| Kim was happy about getting a raise. |
| The guests were interested in hearing about the hotel's services. |

**GRAMMAR NOTE**

Certain adjectives are followed by a preposition. For example, *interested in*: *She's interested in taking a management class.*

**B Look at the adjectives + prepositions in the box. Complete the sentences. Compare answers with a partner.**

| nervous about     tired of     ~~good at~~     proud of     interested in |
| --- |

1. **A:** Is your boss _good at_ giving helpful feedback?

   **B:** No. My boss rates everyone "Needs Improvement."

2. **A:** I'm really _____ being evaluated next week. Reviews make my stomach hurt.

   **B:** Don't worry. Your boss is only _____ helping you. That's what feedback is for.

3. **A:** Aren't you _____ doing the same work every day?

   **B:** Not really. I'm _____ being good at what I do.

**C Write your answers. Then ask and answer the questions with a partner.**

1. What are you interested in learning? _____

2. What are you afraid of doing? _____

3. What do you believe in doing? _____

## 3 Listen for the gerunds to determine the meaning

3-38

**Listen to people talk about Michael. Circle the correct statement.**

1. a. He might try a new career.
   b. He tried a new career.

2. a. He's tired all the time.
   b. He doesn't like his job.

3. a. He'd like to start a business.
   b. He'd like to stay with the restaurant.

4. a. He's spent his money.
   b. He's saved his money.

5. a. His job makes him nervous.
   b. The idea of changing makes him nervous.

6. a. He'll make a decision.
   b. He's made a decision.

## 4 Use gerunds after prepositions to talk about your life experience

**A Think about your answers to these questions.**

1. What are you good at doing?

2. What is one thing you have been thinking about doing but have never done?

3. What is one thing you are tired of doing every day?

4. What are you planning on doing in the future?

5. What's one change you plan on making in the next five years?

**B Work with a partner. Write two more questions.**

1. What is one thing _____ doing?

2. What are you not _____ doing?

**C Work in a team. Ask and answer the questions in 4A and 4B. Take notes on your teammates' answers.**

Laura: *What are you good at doing?*

Micky: *I'm good at photography. What about you?*

Sasha: *I'm pretty good at…*

## ▶▶ TEST YOURSELF

Close your book. Refer to your notes and write six sentences using the information you learned about your classmates. Use a gerund after a preposition in each sentence.

*Micky is good at photography. He's been thinking about going into business as a photographer.*

# 1 Learn ways to participate in a performance review

**A** Listen to the conversation. What positive feedback does Kim hear? What negative feedback does she hear?

3-39

**B** Listen again for the answers. Compare answers with your partner.

3-39

1. What opportunity does the manager offer to Kim?
2. How could the opportunity help her?
3. What does the manager want Kim to do better?
4. What solution does Kim say she will try?

**C** Listen. Write the words Kim uses to respond to the manager's feedback.

3-40

1. Thank you _____ .
2. Oh? I _____ .
3. Of course. _____ .

# 2 Practice your pronunciation

**A** Listen to the sentences. Notice how the words are grouped. (^ = pause)

3-41

I'd suggest asking the supervisor ^ about anything you don't understand.

I was able to help my family ^ and work on my own goals at the same time.

**B** Listen and mark (^) the pauses in these sentences.

3-42

1. I'd like to see some changes ^ in the way you deal with customers.
2. Is a training class for cooks something you'd be interested in?
3. She helps out her co-workers by looking for extra work to do.
4. I've learned a lot about working in a restaurant since I got this job.

**C** Practice the sentences in 2A and 2B with a partner.

## 3 Use polite requests and suggestions with gerunds

**A** Study the chart. What two phrases can you use to make polite requests and suggestions in question form?

| Polite requests and suggestions with gerunds |
| --- |
| I would suggest delivering messages right away. |
| I'd recommend taking a training class. |
| May I suggest getting an earlier bus? |
| Would you mind telling me a little more about the opportunity? |

**B** Work with a partner. Write polite requests or suggestions in the chart in 3A.

1. Apply for a management position.  <u>May I suggest applying for a management position?</u>

2. Give me some more information.  _____

3. Think about your long-term goals.  _____

4. Make a plan to reach your goals.  _____

## 4 Building conversation skills

3-43

**A** Look at the picture and the conversation in 4B. What is the purpose of the conversation? How do you know?

**B** Listen to the sample conversation. How does Luke respond to feedback?

**A:** Well, Luke, you've done a great job of developing new sites, and you make good suggestions for new projects.

**B:** I appreciate your saying so.

**A:** I'd like you to try to be a little more comfortable with asking for help when you need it.

**B:** Oh, I'm sorry. I didn't know there was a problem.

**A:** It's not a big problem. I'd just suggest keeping in mind that your co-workers are here to help if you need them.

**B:** I see. I'll try to do better at asking.

> **IN OTHER WORDS...**
> **Responding to feedback**
> *I appreciate your saying so.*
> *I didn't know there was a problem.*
> *Thanks for saying so.*
> *I didn't realize anything was wrong.*

**C** Role-play the situation below.

| Talk about | Roles | Instructions | Remember |
| --- | --- | --- | --- |
| Discussing performance at work | manager | Your employee keeps the store neat and handles money well. He/She needs to interact more with customers. | Use key phrases from 4B |
| | employee | Listen and respond to the manager's feedback. Commit to improving. | Give and respond to feedback |

AT WORK

## 5 Focus on listening for details

**A Talk about the questions with your class.**

1. What are three things an employer can say to give positive feedback?

2. What are three ways an employer can introduce negative feedback?

**B** 🔊 3-44 **Listen to the speakers. Are the managers giving positive feedback or negative feedback? Check (✓) *Positive feedback* or *Negative feedback*.**

| Positive feedback | Negative feedback | | Positive feedback | Negative feedback |
|---|---|---|---|---|
| 1. | ✓ | 4. | | |
| 2. | | 5. | | |
| 3. | | 6. | | |

**C** 🔊 3-44 **Listen again. Circle the best response.**

1. a. Thank you. I will.
   b. I'm really sorry.

2. a. Thanks. That's good to hear.
   b. I didn't know anything was wrong.

3. a. I appreciate your saying so.
   b. I'll try to do better.

4. a. I'm sorry, but I can't.
   b. I'm sorry.

5. a. Yes, I do.
   b. I didn't know there was a problem.

6. a. I didn't know anything was wrong.
   b. That's wonderful. Thank you.

## 6 Discuss

**A Rank these in order from *1* (most important) to *3* (least important). Work in a group and discuss your rankings.**

- a career you love
- a lot of money
- a lot of time

A: *I think most people would rank having a lot of money number one.*

B: *Hmm. Can you say a little more about why you think so?*

**B Report the results of your discussion to the class.**

*Most of us feel that…. However some people ranked…*

> **SPEAKING NOTE**
>
> **Asking for detail and elaboration**
>
> *Can you say a little more about what you mean by…?*
> *Give us an example of how you think people can…*
> *Can you give me a little more detail on your opinion on…?*

---

## ▶▶ TEST YOURSELF

Assess your participation in the group and class discussions. Today I was able to…

☐ listen effectively        ☐ confirm information and advice
☐ speak accurately          ☐ ask questions

# 1 Read

**A** **Talk about the question with your classmates.**

Why do some jobs have mostly men and some mostly women?

**B** **Read the definitions.**

dominate: (v) control; be the best or most important

eventually: (adv) after some time; after a long time

pioneer: (n) one of the first people to do something

**C** **What can you guess from previewing the article? Circle the answer.**

a. Many women today are chefs and mechanics.

b. Most successful women work in the same fields as their parents.

c. Women can succeed in jobs that are more often held by men.

> **READER'S NOTE**
> Bold headings above sections of text usually summarize the main idea for each section.

**D** **Read the article. What are some examples of nontraditional occupations for women?**

## Breaking the Glass Ceiling: Successful Women in Fields Dominated by Men

The term "glass ceiling" means that in many professions, women may reach a certain level in their careers, but then be unable to advance beyond that level. But with a dream and courage, women are breaking through every day.

### A Pioneering Chef

5 Niki Nakayama grew up in California, where her parents owned a fish-distribution company. She went to culinary school, and eventually became a sushi chef. She opened a sushi café and then, in 2011, a traditional Japanese restaurant in Los Angeles.

10 Nakayama has faced challenges in her career. Female sushi chefs are still unusual, and at Nakayama's first restaurant, a male customer walked out when he saw her behind the sushi bar. In her current restaurant, Nakayama decided not to have an open kitchen. She wants diners at her restaurant to focus on the food, 15 and not on who is making it.

### It's Not Just a Man's World

Another pioneer, Anna Chatten, grew up in Illinois, where her father raced go-karts (small motorized vehicles raced on tracks). When she told her parents that she wanted to race go-karts too, they agreed with one condition: that she maintain and repair them herself. ▼

20 And she's been repairing vehicles ever since. "I can't remember a day when I didn't have tools or didn't know how to use a tool," she says.

Chatten moved to California after high school to attend a school for racing mechanics. "People didn't take me
25 seriously," she says, adding, "I laugh about it now." Today Chatten is one of the few female race-car mechanics in national racing. She loves her job and says she is no different from male race mechanics: "I just happen to be female."

SOURCE: *USA Today*

**E** Read the article again. Are Ms. Nakayama and Ms. Chatten examples of breaking a glass ceiling? Underline the words that support your answer.

**F** In what order did these events happen in Ms. Chatten's life? Number the events from *1* (first) to *5* (now). For each answer, write the line number(s) where you found the answer.

_5_ 1. She is a race car mechanic. (line ____ )

____ 2. She learned to repair go-karts. (line ____ )

____ 3. She faced challenges in earning respect from male mechanics. (line ____ )

____ 4. She completed a training program for mechanics. (line ____ )

____ 5. She became interested in racing. (line ____ )

# 2 Word study

**A** Study the chart. Complete the sentences below.

**Using hyphens to make compound adjectives**

Sometimes two or more words can be joined together by a hyphen (-) to make a compound adjective.

| Words | Compound Adjective |
|---|---|
| one year | one-year training program |
| long term | long-term plans |
| real life | real-life story |
| male dominated | male-dominated world |

1. Ms. Chatten's _long-term_ goal was to become a mechanic.

2. She attended a _____ school for race mechanics.

3. It was difficult at first for her to be accepted in this _____ field.

4. Today, both women are _____ success stories.

**B** Write a sentence about each topic. Use the underlined word in your sentence.

1. a comparison of <u>male-dominated</u> and <u>female-dominated</u> jobs in the U.S. and another country you are familiar with

2. a <u>real-life</u> success story you are familiar with

3. one of your <u>long-term</u> goals

## 3 Talk it over

**A** Look at the graph and read the note. Complete the sentences and answer the questions.

**READER'S NOTE**

A "stacked" bar chart combines data on several areas in one column or row. Labels and a color key help the reader interpret the data.

### Employed people by occupation, sex, race, and Hispanic or Latino ethnicity, 2010

Between 1979 and 2010, the earnings gap between women and men narrowed for most age groups. For 25- to 34-year olds, women earned 68 percent of men's earnings in 1979, but 91 percent of men's earnings in 2010. For 45- to 54-year-olds, women went from earning 57 percent of men's earnings in 1979 to earning 77 percent of men's earnings in 2010.

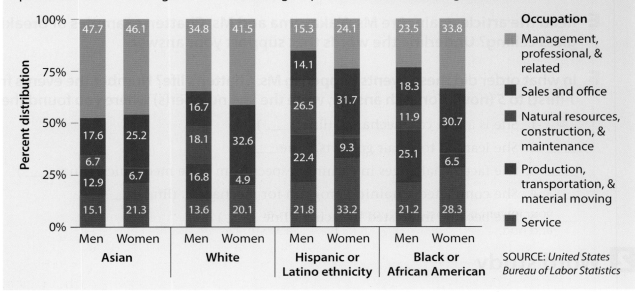

SOURCE: *United States Bureau of Labor Statistics*

1. In which two occupational areas are more women employed than men for all ethnic groups? _____

2. In which occupational area are the fewest women employed? _____

3. In 2010, a woman age 50 earned _____ cents for every dollar earned by a man of the same age.

4. Another word for a difference between earnings is _____ .

5. What information is in the note but not in the graph? _____

**B** Work with a partner to discuss the questions.

1. Should the distribution of ethnicities and women and men in all occupations be more equal? If so, whose responsibility is it to make that change?

2. What are some reasons women may earn less than men?

3. What can people do about earnings gaps?

---

## ⏻ BRING IT TO LIFE

Use the public library or the Internet to find an article with a short biography (life story) of an interesting person. Bring the biography to class and talk about the person's achievements with your group.

**A** Listen to the staff meeting. What are they discussing?

3-45

**B** Listen to the staff meeting again. Then put a check next to each idea or suggestion that is mentioned.

3-45

_____ tell employees about things that are happening

_____ ask employees to tell other employees important information

_____ put important information in writing

_____ make suggestions to supervisors

_____ consider everyone's ideas equal

**C** Listen again. Which ideas do you agree with? Talk about your ideas with a partner.

3-45

**D** Read the chart. Discuss the questions below with your class.

| When you want to agree with someone you can | |
| --- | --- |
| **Do this** | **Say this** |
| • Nod your head up and down.<br>• Smile and nod.<br>• Tilt your head to one side and push your lower lip up into your upper lip, and nod. | I agree.<br>I agree 100%.<br>I completely agree.<br>True!<br>Absolutely!<br>You're right! |

1. Does nodding with a smile have a different meaning than nodding without a smile? When would you nod with a smile? Without a smile?

2. What else can you say to show that you agree with someone?

3. In a formal situation, what should you not do to show that you agree?

**E** Work with a partner. Take turns reading the issues. Talk about the consequences of each situation. Make suggestions to improve each situation.

Supervisors don't ask employees for suggestions to solve problems.

Employees believe that supervisors aren't interested in hearing suggestions.

Employees and supervisors are from different cultures and have different expectations about work.

**F** Have a staff meeting.

1. Work with a group to make a list of communication or collaboration issues at work.

2. Choose one person to facilitate a focus group. Take turns making suggestions on the issues on this page.

A: *What are some other things that cause communication problems?*

B: *My supervisor never...I would like to..., but...*

C: *What do you think would happen if you tried...?*

**A** Collaborate to write a review of Delia's Restaurant. It can be positive or negative. Include gerunds with the phrases in the box in your review.

The staff of Delia's Restaurant believes in creating an experience for every customer. The Maitre d' likes seating everyone himself.

believe in
interested in
great at
get an award for
proud of
tired of
instead of
nervous about
contribute to
recommend

**B** Complete the email. Use the verbs in parentheses. Compare emails with your team.

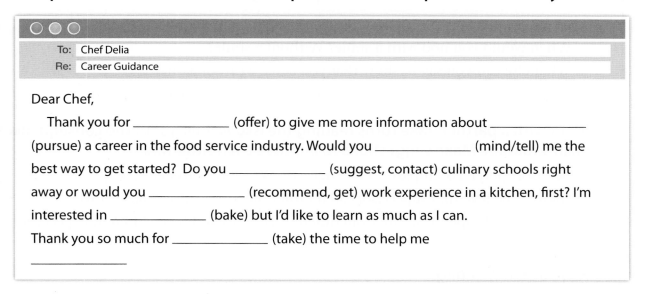

To: Chef Delia
Re: Career Guidance

Dear Chef,

Thank you for _____ (offer) to give me more information about _____ (pursue) a career in the food service industry. Would you _____ (mind/tell) me the best way to get started? Do you _____ (suggest, contact) culinary schools right away or would you _____ (recommend, get) work experience in a kitchen, first? I'm interested in _____ (bake) but I'd like to learn as much as I can.

Thank you so much for _____ (take) the time to help me _____

**C** Imagine you can interview someone else with an interesting career. Collaborate to write at least five questions you would like to ask. Use the phrases in the box.

*Would you mind describing your day at the office?*

| | |
|---|---|
| Would you mind… | Would you suggest… |
| What would you recommend… | How should I go about… |

**D** Take turns role-playing an informational interview using your questions from C.

**E** **Work in a team. Follow the steps below to complete the task.**

1. Assign team roles: manager, writer, editor, actors.

2. Choose one of the pictures on the right.

3. Write a conversation for the people in the picture. Model the leadership qualities from Lesson 1.

4. Rehearse your conversation. Act it out for the class.

**F** **Interview three classmates. Write their answers.**

1. Name someone you think is really successful. What has that person achieved?

2. What is one achievement of yours that your classmates probably don't know about? When did it happen?

3. Name one leadership quality that you would like to work on developing. Why did you choose this quality?

**G** **Report your results for Exercise F, #2 to the class. Make a time line of your classmates' achievements.**

## PROBLEM SOLVING

3-46
**A** **Listen and read about Jafari.**

When Jafari immigrated to the U.S. twelve years ago, he had a lot of dreams. Life wasn't easy at first. He worked two jobs and didn't have much time to work on his goals. But over time, things got easier. Jafari was able to go through a training program at the local college, find a good job, and finally buy a house for his family.

Today, Jafari owns his own business and is proud of everything he's accomplished. Now that he has a little more free time, he's interested in giving something back to the community. He'd like to be involved in something that would really make his community a better place to live, but he doesn't know where to start.

**B** **Work with your classmates. Respond to the prompts.**

1. Identify Jafari's problem.

2. Make a list of things Jafari could do to start getting involved. Discuss the pros and cons (arguments for and arguments against) each idea.

## Action verbs in the simple present

| Statements | |
|---|---|
| I<br>You | work. |
| He<br>She<br>It | works. |
| We<br>They | work. |

| Negative statements | | |
|---|---|---|
| I<br>You | don't | |
| He<br>She<br>It | doesn't | work. |
| We<br>They | don't | |

| Note |
|---|
| Most verbs describe actions.<br>These verbs are called action verbs. |

| Yes/No questions | | |
|---|---|---|
| Do | I<br>you | |
| Does | he<br>she<br>it | work? |
| Do | we<br>they | |

| Answers | | | | | | | |
|---|---|---|---|---|---|---|---|
| Yes, | I<br>you | do. | | No, | I<br>you | don't. |
| | he<br>she<br>it | does. | | | he<br>she<br>it | doesn't. |
| | we<br>they | do. | | | we<br>they | don't. |

## Action verbs in the present continuous

| Affirmative statements | |
|---|---|
| I'm<br>You're<br>He's<br>She's<br>It's<br>We're<br>They're | working. |

| Negative statements | |
|---|---|
| I'm<br>You're<br>He's<br>She's<br>It's<br>We're<br>They're | not working. |

## Stative verbs

| Some stative verbs | | |
|---|---|---|
| be | like | seem |
| believe | love | smell |
| dislike | mean | sound |
| forget | need | taste |
| have | own | think |
| hear | possess | understand |
| include | remember | want |
| know | see | |

| Note |
|---|
| Use stative verbs to describe feelings, knowledge, beliefs, and the senses. Stative verbs are usually not used in the present continuous. |

# Types of questions

| Yes/No questions and answers |
| --- |
| A: Do you agree? |
| B: Yes, I do. OR No, I don't. |

| Information questions and answers |
| --- |
| A: Who agrees with you? |
| B: Everyone agrees with me. |

| Or questions and answers |
| --- |
| A: Do they agree or disagree? |
| B: They agree. |

| Direct information questions |
| --- |
| When will the mayor be here? |
| Where is the meeting? |
| What does the mayor want? |
| How did you hear about it? |
| Why did they call a meeting? |

| Indirect information questions |
| --- |
| Do you know when the mayor will be here? |
| Could you tell me where the meeting is? |
| Do you know what the mayor wants? |
| Can you tell me how you heard about it? |
| Do you know why they called a meeting? |

| Note |
| --- |
| Indirect questions sound more polite than Yes/No or information questions. |

## Yes/No question with *if* or *whether*

| Direct | Answers | | |
| --- | --- | --- | --- |
| Did they discuss the issue? | Can you tell me | if / whether | they discussed the issue? |
| | Could you tell me | | |
| | Do you know | | |

## Tag questions and short answers with *be*

| Affirmative statement | Negative tag | Agreement | Disagreement |
| --- | --- | --- | --- |
| You're new, | aren't you? | Yes, I am. | No, I'm not. |
| The manager was here, | wasn't she? | Yes, she was. | No, she wasn't. |
| The books are old, | aren't they? | Yes, they are. | No, they're not. |

| Negative statement | Affirmative tag | Agreement | Disagreement |
| --- | --- | --- | --- |
| You're not busy, | are you? | No, I'm not. | Yes, I am. |
| The manager wasn't here, | was she? | No, she wasn't. | Yes, she was. |
| He isn't coming in today, | is he? | No, he isn't. | Yes, he is. |

| Notes |
| --- |
| • Use a negative tag after an affirmative statement. Negative tags are usually contracted. Ask a negative tag question when you expect the answer to be "Yes." |
| • Use an affirmative tag after a negative statement. Ask an affirmative tag question when you expect the answer to be "No." |

## Tag questions and short answers with *do* and *did*

| Affirmative statement | Negative tag | Agreement | Disagreement |
| --- | --- | --- | --- |
| The landlord fixed it, | didn't he? | Yes, he did. | No, he didn't. |
| The heat works, | doesn't it? | Yes, it does. | No, it doesn't. |
| They emailed, | didn't they? | Yes, they did. | No, they didn't. |

| Negative statement | Affirmative tag | | Agreement | Disagreement |
|---|---|---|---|---|
| The landlord didn't fix it, | did he? | | No, he didn't. | Yes, he did. |
| The heat doesn't work, | does it? | | No, it doesn't. | Yes, it does. |
| They didn't email, | did they? | | No, they didn't. | Yes, they did. |

## The past passive

| Negative statements | | | Notes |
|---|---|---|---|
| I | was | | • The past passive uses the verbs *was/were* + the past participle: The road **was closed**. |
| You | were | | • We use the active voice to say what people or things do or did: They **closed** the road. |
| He She It | was | taken to the hospital. | • The passive voice directs the action toward the subject. |
| We They | were | | • The active voice directs the action toward an object.<br>• We use the passive voice when we do not know who performed the action, when it is not important who performed the action, or when it is clear who performed the action. |

| *Yes/No* question and short answers | Information question and answer |
|---|---|
| **A:** Were they taken to the hospital? | **A:** Where were they taken? |
| **B:** Yes, they were. OR<br>**B:** No, they weren't. | **B:** They were taken to City Hospital. |

## Reflexive pronouns

| Subject pronoun | Reflexive pronoun | Notes |
|---|---|---|
| I | myself | • Reflexive pronouns end with *-self* or *-selves*. |
| you | yourself | • Use a reflexive pronoun when the subject and object of the sentence refer to the same person, people, or thing. She saw **herself** on TV. |
| he | himself | • Use *by* + reflexive pronoun to say that someone or something is alone or does something without help from others.<br>I watched TV by **myself**. |
| she | herself | |
| it | itself | |
| we | ourselves | |
| you | yourselves | |
| they | themselves | |

## Reported speech

| Quoted speech statement | | Reported speech statement | | Reported speech with *told* + noun or pronoun | |
|---|---|---|---|---|---|
| I<br>You<br>He<br>She<br>It<br>We<br>They | said, "It's OK." | I<br>You<br>He<br>She<br>It<br>We<br>They | said (that) it was OK. | I<br>You<br>He<br>She<br>It<br>We<br>They | told me (that) it was OK. |

- Use quoted speech to repeat exactly what a person said or wrote.
- Use reported speech to tell what someone has said or written.
- For quoted speech in the simple present, the reported speech is in the simple past.
- For quoted speech in the present continuous, the reported speech is in the past continuous.
- Use *said* to report a person's words.
- Use *told* to report on who heard the words. Use a noun (someone's name) or an object pronoun (*me, you, her, him, us, you, them*) after *told*.

| Quoted speech instruction | | Reported speech instruction | | Notes |
|---|---|---|---|---|
| I<br>You<br>He<br>She<br>It<br>We<br>They | said, "Stop."<br>said, "Don't wait." | I<br>You<br>He<br>She<br>It<br>We<br>They | told me to stop.<br>said to stop.<br>told me not to wait.<br>said not to wait. | • Use an infinitive (*to* + verb or *not to* + verb) to report an instruction. |

## The past perfect

| Affirmative statements | | | Negative statements | | | Contraction |
|---|---|---|---|---|---|---|
| I<br>You<br>He<br>She<br>It<br>We<br>They | had left | before the rain started. | I<br>You<br>He<br>She<br>It<br>We<br>They | had not left | before the rain started. | had not = hadn't |

**Notes**

- The past perfect uses *had/had not* + past participle
- Use the past perfect to show that an event happened before another event in the past. The past perfect shows the earlier event:
  When Ms. Porter interviewed Luis, she had prepared some questions.
  = First Ms. Porter prepared some questions. Then she interviewed Luis.

| *Yes/No* questions | | | | Answers | | | | | | |
|---|---|---|---|---|---|---|---|---|---|---|
| Had | I<br>you<br>he<br>she<br>it<br>we<br>they | left | before the rain started? | Yes, | I<br>you<br>he<br>she<br>it<br>we<br>they | had. | No, | I<br>you<br>he<br>she<br>it<br>we<br>they | hadn't. |

| Information questions | | | | Answers | |
|---|---|---|---|---|---|
| How long had | I<br>you<br>he<br>she<br>it<br>we<br>they | waited | before the bus came? | I<br>You<br>He<br>She<br>It<br>We<br>They | had waited for an hour before the bus came. |

## Adjective clauses

| Main clause | Adjective clause after main clause | |
|---|---|---|
| I like working with people | who | work hard. |
| | that | |
| I can solve problems | that | happen in my job. |
| | which | |

| Note |
|---|
| Use adjective clauses to give more information about a noun in the main clause of the sentence. |

| Main clause | | | |
|---|---|---|---|
| Adjective clause inside main clause | | | |
| The supervisor | who/that | hired me | likes my work. |
| The work | which/that | I do | is done well. |

| Main clause | Adjective clause with *whose* |
|---|---|
| I am the employee | whose paycheck was lost. |
| They are the people | whose children we saw. |

| Note |
|---|
| Adjective clauses with *whose* show who something belongs to. |

## Statements with *wh-* and *if/whether* phrases

| Main clause | Phrase with *wh-* or *if/whether* |
|---|---|
| I'm not sure | **when** the meeting starts. |
| She doesn't know | **where** the meeting will be held. |
| They have no idea | **what** the meeting is about. |
| I can't remember | **if** they're going to discuss the issue. |
| He wonders | **whether** they'll discuss the budget. |

| Note |
|---|
| Use a *wh-* or *if/whether* phrase after certain expressions to talk about things you don't know for certain. |

## Present unreal conditional

| Statements | |
|---|---|
| **If clause** | **Main clause** |
| If I worked hard, | I could get a better job. |
| If she got a better job, | she would be happier. |
| If they spent less, | they could save for college. |

| Notes |
|---|
| • Use unreal conditionals to talk about unreal, untrue, or impossible situations. |
| • In unreal conditionals, the *if* clause can also come after the main clause:<br>She would be happier if she got a better job. |

| *Yes/No* question and short answers | |
|---|---|
| **A:** Would you work if you didn't need the money? | **B:** No, I wouldn't. |
| **A:** If she wanted a better job, would she go to college? | **B:** Yes, she would. |
| **A:** If they had a car, would they drive to work? | **B:** Yes, they would. |

| *Information questions and answers* | |
|---|---|
| **A:** Where would you work if you could work anywhere? | **B:** I would work at the college. |
| **A:** If you could have any job, what job would you have? | **B:** I would own a business. |

| Statements with be | |
|---|---|
| **If clause** | **Main clause** |
| If I were you, | I would ask for help. |

**Note**

In formal speech with present unreal conditions, use *were* for all people (*if I were…, if you were…, if he were…, if she were…, if they were…*).

## Adverbs of degree

| Least | | | Most or greatest |
|---|---|---|---|
| I am a little tired. | I am pretty tired. | I am really tired. | I am extremely tired. |
| I am somewhat tired. | I am fairly tired. | I am very tired. | |

## So, such, and that

| *So…that, such…that,* and *such a/an…that* | |
|---|---|
| The store is **so** popular | |
| The store has **such** low prices | **that** it is always crowded. |
| It is **such a** small store | |

**Notes**

- Use *so, such, such a/an + that* to show a result.
- Use *so* with an adverb or an adjective.
- Use *such* or *such a/an* with an adjective + a singular count noun.

## Advice and necessity

| Should, had better, and ought to | | |
|---|---|---|
| You | should shouldn't | stay home today. |
| | had better had better not | |
| | ought to | |

**Notes**

- Use *should* and *ought to* to give advice. They mean the same thing.
- *Have to, have got to, had better* and *must* are often used to give strong advice.
- *Have got to* is as strong as *have to* and *must*, but is less formal.
- In informal conversations, people often say "You better" instead of "You'd better."

| Advice and strong advice | | |
|---|---|---|
| Mildest | should shouldn't ought to | You **should** see a doctor. You **shouldn't** go to work. You **ought to** see a doctor. |
| | had better had better not | You'**d better** see a doctor. You'**d better** not go to work. |
| Strongest | have to have got to must | You **have to** see a doctor. You'**ve got to** see a doctor. You **must** see a doctor. |

**Note**

- In the U. S., people don't usually use *ought to* in a negative statement.

| Confirming advice | | |
|---|---|---|
| So I | should | stay home today. |
| | shouldn't | |
| | need to | |
| | am supposed to | |
| | have to | |

# Necessity in the past

| Present | | | | Past | | | | Note |
|---|---|---|---|---|---|---|---|---|
| I<br>You<br>He<br>She<br>It | have to<br>have got to<br>*must*<br>has to<br>has got to<br>*must* | stop. | | I<br>You<br>He<br>She<br>It<br>We<br>They | had to | stop. | | There are no past forms of *must* or *have got to*. Use *had to* instead. |
| We<br>They | have to<br>have got to<br>*must* | | | | | | | |

# Past of *should*

| Affirmative statements | | | | Negative statements | | | | Contraction |
|---|---|---|---|---|---|---|---|---|
| I<br>You<br>He<br>She<br>It<br>We<br>They | should have | stopped. | | You<br>He<br>She<br>It<br>We<br>They | should not have | stopped. | | should not = shouldn't |

**Note**

Use *should (not) have* + past participle to give an opinion about a situation in the past.

# Gerunds and infinitives

| Verb + Gerund | Verb + Infinitive | Note |
|---|---|---|
| She avoids exercising. | She decided to exercise. | Some verbs (start, continue, like, prefer) can be used with a gerund or an infinitive. |
| He quit exercising. | He agrees to exercise. | |
| I'd consider exercising. | I plan to exercise. | |
| They feel like exercising. | They need to exercise. | |
| I started exercising. | I started to exercise. | |
| He'll continue exercising. | He'll continue to exercise. | |
| She likes exercising. | She likes to exercise. | |
| They prefer exercising. | They prefer to exercise. | |

| Preposition + gerund | Notes |
|---|---|
| She does a good job **of solving** problems. | • Gerunds are used after prepositions like *about, at, for, in, instead of,* and *to.* |
| She knows a lot **about answering** the phone. | • Gerunds are also used after verb phrases with prepositions: *She cares about helping people.* |
| She is good **at taking** phone messages. | |
| **Instead of getting** a raise, she got a promotion. | |

## Gerund after *be* + adjective + preposition

She is interested **in learning** about the review.

They are proud **of getting** raises.

We are known **for offering** English for Health Careers classes.

I am happy **about going** to this class.

### Note

Certain adjectives are almost always followed by a preposition. *She is interested in helping people.*

## Polite requests and suggestions with verbs and gerunds

I would suggest **applying** for a management position.

May I recommend **planning** a visit to the career center?

Would you mind **giving** us more time?

# Prefixes, suffixes, and endings

## The suffix *-less*

harmless = not harmful

speechless = unable to speak

wireless = without a wire

### Note

Add *-less* to some nouns to form adjectives. *-less* usually means "without" or "not".

## The suffixes *-er* and *-ee*

| Verb | Noun | Noun |
|------|------|------|
| employ | employer | employee |
| train | trainer | trainee |
| pay | payer | payee |

### Notes

- The suffix *-er* indicates the person who performs an action.
- The suffix *-ee* indicates the person who receives the result of the action. A *trainer* trains a *trainee.*

## The suffix *-ous*

| Noun | Adjective |
|------|-----------|
| caution | cautious |
| danger | dangerous |
| hazard | hazardous |

### Note

Add *-ous* to some nouns to form adjectives. Note that spelling might change; for example, caution—cautious.

## The suffixes *-ed* and *-ing*

| | |
|------|------|
| disappointed | disappointing |
| interested | interesting |
| confused | confusing |

### Notes

- Adjectives ending in *-ed* describe a person's feelings: He was bored.
- Adjectives ending in *-ing* describe the cause of the feelings: The job was boring.

## The suffix *-ful*

| Noun | Adjective |
|------|-----------|
| help | helpful |
| care | careful |
| beauty | beautiful |

### Note

Add *-ful* to some nouns to form adjectives. *-ful* usually means full of. Note that spelling might change; for example, beauty—beautiful.

## The suffix -*ment*

| Verb | Noun |
|---|---|
| agree | agreement |
| announce | announcement |
| assign | assignment |

**Note**

Add -*ment* to some verbs to form nouns.

## Prefixes for negative forms of adjectives

| Adjective | Negative form |
|---|---|
| responsible | irresponsible |
| flexible | inflexible |
| reliable | unreliable |
| honest | dishonest |

**Note**

Add the prefixes *dis-*, *in-*, *ir-*, and *un-* to some adjectives to make negative forms.

## The suffix -*ize*

| Adjective or noun | verb |
|---|---|
| strategy | strategize |
| equal | equalize |
| character | characterize |

**Note**

The suffix -*ize* means to cause something to become something.

## The suffix -*ity*

| Adjective | Noun |
|---|---|
| active | activity |
| able | ability |
| similar | similarity |
| major | majority |

**Note**

The suffix -*ity* means a quality or condition. Add -*ity* to some adjectives to make a related noun.

## The prefix *re-*

| Verb | Verb |
|---|---|
| do | redo |
| apply | reapply |
| write | rewrite |
| enter | re-enter |

**Note**

The prefix *re-* usually means *again* or *back*. Words with *re-* sometimes have a hyphen if the first letter after the prefix is a vowel.

## Compound adjectives

| Words | Compound adjective |
|---|---|
| one year | one-year training class |
| long term | long-term plans |
| real life | real-life story |
| well known | well-known author |

**Note**

Using hyphens to make compound adjectives. Sometimes two or more words can be joined together by a hyphen (-) to make a compound adjective.

## OXFORD
UNIVERSITY PRESS

198 Madison Avenue
New York, NY 10016 USA

Great Clarendon Street, Oxford, OX2 6DP, United Kingdom

Oxford University Press is a department of the University of Oxford.
It furthers the University's objective of excellence in research, scholarship,
and education by publishing worldwide. Oxford is a registered trade
mark of Oxford University Press in the UK and in certain other countries

© Oxford University Press 2017

The moral rights of the author have been asserted

First published in 2017

2025 2024 2023 2022

10 9 8 7

ISBN: 9 78 0 19 449281 2 Student Book (Pack)

ISBN: 9 78 0 19 449304 8 Student Book (Pack Component)

ISBN: 9 78 0 19 449284 3 Online Practice (Pack Component)

ISBN: 9 78 0 19 440479 2 OEVT App

Printed in China

This book is printed on paper from certified and well-managed sources

ACKNOWLEDGMENTS

*Back cover photograph*: Oxford University Press building/David Fisher

*The publisher is grateful to those who have given permission to reproduce the following
extracts and adaptations of copyright material:*

The Media Insight Project - an initiative of the American Press Institute and
the Associated Press - NORC Center for Public Affairs Research"

"Job Outlook 2015." Reprinted from the 2015 Job Outlook, with permission of
the National Association of Colleges and Employers, copyright holder.

"Meet 3 Successful Women in Fields Dominated by Men" from USA Today,
2013-11-28 ©2013 Gannett – USA Today. All rights reserved. Used by
permission and protected by the Copyright Laws of the United States. The
printing, copying, redistribution, or retransmission of this Context without
express written permission is prohibited."

*Illustrations by*: Cover, Jeff Mangiat / Mendola Artist Representatives; 5W
Infographics, p. 16, p. 43, p. 48, p. 64, p. 78, p. 80, p. 96, p. 112, p. 128, p. 164,
p. 165, p. 192; Joe "Fearless" Arenella/Will Sumpter, p. 195; Shawn Banner, p.
56, p. 60; Barb Bastian, p. 53, p. 155; John Batten, p. 13, p. 72, p. 125; Arlene
Boehm, p. 22; Molly Borman-Pullman, p. 139, p. 146; Laurie Conley, p. 104, p.
136; Phil Constansinesco, p. 6, p. 29, p. 75; Ken Dewar, p. 117; Bill Dickson,
p. 59, p. 121, p. 156, p. 187; Mike Gardner, p. 3, p. 68, p. 108, p. 156; Garth
Glazier/AA Reps, p. 50; Steve Graham, p.146 (top); Glenn Gustafson, p. 82, p.
162; Mark Hannon, p. 37, p. 85;; Ben Hasler/NB Illustration, p. 34, p. 108; Janos
Jantner, p. 27, p. 51, p. 76, p. 92; p. 123, p. 156, p. 194; Uldis Klavins, p. 36, p.
68; John Kurtz, p. 5, p. 28, p. 40, p. 124, p. 141, p. 173; Jeffrey Lindberg, p.130;
Deb Lofaso, p. 5, p. 14, p. 20, p. 21, p. 24, p. 30, p. 32, p. 38, p. 39, p. 46, p. 52,
p. 53, p. 62, p. 69, p. 72, p. 91, p. 93, p. 94, p. 100 (right), p. 110, p. 126, p. 132,
p. 134, p. 141, p. 142, p. 144, p. 158, p. 159, p. 174, p. 184, p. 190, p. 191; Karen
Minot, p. 21, p. 69; Tom Newsom, p. 180; Geo Parkin, p. 8, p. 11, p. 25, p. 32, p.
38, p. 99, p. 120, p. 140, p. 174; Terry Pazcko, p. 98; Aaron Sacco, p. 12, p. 88,
p. 100 (left), p. 107, p. 108 (top), p. 148, p. 172, p. 188; Ben Shannon/Magnet
Reps, p.130; Jane Spencer, p. 2, p. 152; Ralph Voltz/Deborah Wolfe,
p. 66; Jeff Wack/Mendola Art, p.114; Patrick Welsh, p. 19, p. 168, p. 171; Simon
Williams/Illustration Ltd., p. 18; Craig Zuckerman, p. 147.

*We would also like to thank the following for permission to reproduce the following
photographs:* Click Bestsellers / Shutterstock.com, Cover; Hero Images/
Getty Images, p. 10 (students); Caiaimage/Sam Edwards/Getty Images, p.
14 (student); Carlo Allegri/Reuters, p. 20 (United Nations); Margo Harrison/
Shutterstock.com, p. 20 (cowboy); anouchka/Getty Images, p. 20 (couple at
café); Getty Images, p. 20 (baseball player); Hero Images Inc./Alamy Stock
Photo, p. 21 (bus driver and passenger); Robert Landau/Alamy Stock Photo,
p. 21 (traffic); Denis Balibouse/Reuters, p. 24 (car accident); Tetra Images/
Alamy Stock Photo, p. 42 (woman driving); ARENA Creative/Shutterstock.
com, p. 44 (women talking); MShieldsPhotos/Alamy Stock Photo, p. 46 (bikes);
Phovoir/Shutterstock.com, p. 52 (work meeting); MBI/Alamy Stock Photo, p.
61 (women working); REUTERS/Alamy Stock Photo, p. 74 (vegetable market);
DreamPictures/Getty Images, p. 77 (newscasters); Cheryl Savan/Shutterstock.
com, p. 81 (man with sign); Monty Rakusen/Getty Images, p. 94 (training
course graduates); simonkr/Getty Images, p. 106 (students walking); Roy Hsu/
Getty Images, p. 110 (businesswoman); David Litman/Shutterstock.com, p. 122
(roller coaster); Echo/Getty Images, p. 124 (woman shopping); Brad Rickerby/
Getty Images, p. 132 (old woman); Aurora Photos/Alamy Stock Photo, p. 134
(woman jumping); Martin Wierink/Alamy Stock Photo, p. 138 (sick woman);
Susan Vogel/Getty Images, p. 142 (woman paying bills); Lyudmila Tetera/
Shutterstock.com, p. 158 (garbage); RosaIreneBetancourt 5/Alamy Stock
Photo, p. 159 (meeting); UpperCut Images/Alamy Stock Photo, p. 164 (couple
buying house); Gary Burchell/Getty Images, p. 179 (work colleagues); Syda
Productions/Shutterstock.com, p. 181 (woman working); cozyta/Shutterstock.
com, p. 186 (photographer); Ascent Xmedia/Getty Images, p. 186 (mountain
climber); Claudia Totir/Getty Images, p. 190 (sushi); Cal Sport Media/Alamy
Stock Photo, p. 191 (car racing).